NORTH EAST CASTLES

NORTH EAST CASTLES

Castles in the Landscape of North East Scotland

edited by
JOHN S. SMITH

ABERDEEN UNIVERSITY PRESS
Member of Maxwell Macmillan Pergamon Publishing Corporation

First published 1990
Aberdeen University Press

© Aberdeen University Press for the collected works 1990

British Library Cataloguing in Publication Data
North east castles : castles in the landscape of North East
    Scotland.
    1. Scotland. Castles
    I. Smith, J. S. (John Smart)
    941.1

    ISBN 0-08-040931-8

Typeset from author generated discs by
Hewer Text Composition Services, Edinburgh
and printed by Billing & Sons Ltd., Worcester.

CONTENTS

ILLUSTRATIONS

Access: many of the castles described in this volume are open to the public or visible from a public road. Some, however, are privately owned, and readers are requested to respect the occupiers' privacy.

PREFACE

This is the fifth collection of papers to be published based on the local history day conference organised by the Centre for Scottish Studies and the Centre for Continuing Education of the University of Aberdeen. The conference held on 4 November, 1989 attracted a large support of castle buffs and was distinguished by the range of approaches presented towards increasing our understanding of these distinctive emblems of our historic past. The increasing public interest in heritage appreciation and conservation of castles here in the North East is reflected in the inclusion of papers by Aboyne-based stone mason Alistair Urquhart on castle restoration, and by Colin Coutts assessing restoration compromises adopted from an architectural/historical viewpoint. The latter piece of work was completed after the conference had taken place but is included here because it complements the different approaches to the castle in the landscape revealed by the conference papers. Thanks are due to the authors of the papers for allowing them to be published; to Jim Livingston of the Department of Geography and Alistair Urquhart for the photographic illustrations; to Rod Gunson, the Centre's Conference Organiser, and staff of the Department of Continuing Education, for their hard work behind the scenes; and to Dr Grant Simpson, who not only chaired the morning and afternoon sessions of the conference, but also contributed an introduction to this volume.

JOHN S. SMITH
Director of the Centre for Scottish Studies
and Senior Lecturer in Geography
University of Aberdeen

INTRODUCTION

Grant G. Simpson

The tradition of study of the castles of North East Scotland is ancient and honourable: works on the topic by Sir Andrew Leith Hay and James Giles appeared in early Victorian times. And the principal expositor of the subject in the 20th century, Dr W. Douglas Simpson, devoted an amazing amount of erudition and energy to discussing in lecture and in print these, his favourite buildings.

Yet in spite of all the attention which has been given to this large and fascinating group of castles, there is still much to be learned from them. Dr Simpson himself was a pioneer in applying archaeological techniques to constructions which all too often had been seen in terms of architectural history alone. Throughout a long life of scholarship he never failed to emphasise the need to employ documentary and physical evidence in conjunction. A sense of the vital importance of a comprehensive approach in castle studies has similarly produced a new word for the subject, invented by French scholars: castellologie. While rather lacking in emphony, the term encapsulates an essential idea. The series of international conferences under the title *Chateau Gaillard* which was presided over from 1962 to 1988 by the late Professor Michel de Boüard had as its aim, in his words: 'stimuler et faire connaître des études enterprises avec les moyens propre de l'archéologie, mais dans une perspective historique, sur les lieux fortifiés du moyen age'. What, then, are the wider contexts into which we need to put our castles? An archaeological background is required, in the very fullest sense. More attention is needed, not merely to the archaeology in and immediately adjacent to the buildings themselves, but also to the physical recovery of early landscapes and settlement patterns. Our surviving stone castles, by virtue of their relatively durable materials, have become largely divorced

1

from their original surroundings. Tower houses especially tend to impress us as free-standing erections. To respect their original state in its completeness requires more investigation of medieval rural archaeology than is yet being given, as a rule. The task of locating and describing villages, field patterns and routeways is far from easy, but these were features essentially related to castles, which served as the administrative, economic and social centres of the landed estates which surrounded them. A few Scottish historians have pointed to the significance of such topics (e.g. A.A.M. Duncan, *Scotland: the Making of the Kingdom*, 1975, 433–43), but on the whole, our archaeologists are lagging behind.

The domestic background of the castle has sometimes received less emphasis than its military purposes. Mr Geoffrey Stell has underlined the faulty logic in the assumption that there was 'a process of Darwinian-like evolution in which the medieval castle is transformed through a semi-fortified stage into the recognisably modern home . . . The transformation is taken at its face value as an accurate, visible reflection of a corresponding "improvement" in the behaviour and outlook of "warlike" medieval man' (in K.J. Stringer, ed., *Essays on the Nobility of Medieval Scotland*, 1985, 196). Yet he also rightly points out that the residential aspect of these 'multi-purpose buildings' had great importance for their inhabitants. Spells of active involvement in active warfare represented a very limited period of time overall in the history of a castle. For the remainder people had to live their normal lives in it, as best they could. Documentary information on that element tends to be very scanty in the medieval period at least. But more could be done by useful analysis to illuminate daily castle living. Were the inhabitants of castles troubled by the fact that much of the food they ate was only half-heated? 'Because of the difficulty of disposing of smoke and smells, a great deal of cooking was almost certainly done out in the open when weather permitted . . . The food was unlikely to arrive very hot at the table after traversing the draughty courtyards or being carried up spiral stone staircases' (John Burke, *Life in the Castle in Medieval England*, 1978, 39). The point may seem in itself of minor significance, but the necessity of grasping the daily realities of castle living must be emphasised.

Another feature of the castle in its original environment is perhaps even more difficult to grasp—its symbolism. These structures were put there by the top men of medieval society and there is no doubt that they were intended to look correspondingly impressive. Mr Stell has remarked that 'castle walls and towers . . . convey an impression of height for height's sake, a symbolic attribute that doubtless accounts for the enduring popularity of the tower house' (in Stringer, op.cit., 201). Anyone who has climbed from a Swiss valley up its hillside and then to the top of its local castle will readily appreciate that the building was designed not only to be secure but also to dominate visually the inhabitants below. Study of the symbolism of castles is greatly needed, but will require careful investigation: scholarly reconstruction drawings, study of sight-lines and especially an attempt to discover the original ecological state of the surrounding landscape.

We also have to think more clearly and fully about the context in which our castles exist at the present day. We have to be reminded, for example, that, even more so than other buildings, they are not totally solid, immobile constructions which merely last for ever. Castles, like houses, are on the move: a slate comes off here, a piece of harling cracks there, and a spot of damp creeps through in some invisible corner. These are the realms which rightly concern the building craftsmen and the castle restorer, as Mr Alistair Urquhart and Mr Marc Ellington demonstrate in their contributions which follow. In addition to preservation, nowadays presentation also demands a fully professional approach with the pressures of the tourist boom and the heritage industry. All ancient monuments have acquired a more demanding function in our own generation: satisfying public enthusiasm for observing and trying to understand the past. All this can readily result in conflicting calls made upon a building or site. Preservation experts are seriously worried by the erosion of the wooden floors and rural footpaths caused by the incessant tramp of tourist feet. Conveying both atmosphere and instructional data in a castle presents difficulties, as one example will illustrate. At Crathes Castle, the insistence of the National Trust for Scotland on subdued 'original-level' lighting has meant that in some rooms the visitor cannot effectively see what he has come to inspect. A clash of intentions has produced a problem: and the Trust should re-think its lighting scheme at that particular property. Castles have an endless fascination, but to appreciate them fully we must depend on the efforts of those who are expert, not only on the past itself, but also increasingly, on the past in the present.

ROOM AT THE TOP—FROM CASTLE TO DEFENSIBLE RESIDENCE

John S. Smith

A castle may be popularly defined as a fortified house or fortress, the residence of a prince or nobleman, or a large country mansion generally.[1] In its historical origins, the concept of a castle developed throughout Europe in an attempt to protect civilised life from 'barbarians' like the Vikings. The earliest seeds were sown in the Early European Iron Age where first palisaded enclosures, and then hillforts and brochs were spawned in an increasingly militarised landscape, driven by a progressively hostile environment, population growth and immigration from around 600 BC onwards. As later in historical time, these defensive structures were devised by a society under pressure from invasion, shortage of land and social change. Groupings in the Scottish Iron Age numbered at the most several hundred souls, with the latest ideas for North Scottish brochs involving the tower as the centrepiece in a village of round and oval houses as at Jarlshof, Gurness and Midhowe in the Northern Isles.[2] Here apparently the elements of home and fortress were already juxtaposed, although not in the same building. The presence of internal scarcement ledges and intramural staircases in a work almost exclusively of stone invites the possibility, in at least a few brochs, of several levels of occupation, and certainly an appreciation of the advantages of height and fire-proof walls against the offensive weapons of the sling and fire javelin. In the North East of Scotland, hillforts appear to have fulfilled a similar role to brochs and duns in a less broken terrain, where maritime matters were of less moment. The size of the multi-vallate stone and timber defences appears to have been determined by the contours of the chosen hill top. Lack of modern hillfort excavation makes it impossible to state with certainty that hillforts were permanently occupied. Those hillforts which were sited at considerable elevations above sea level were

5

probably not permanently occupied but their presence attests the ability of Iron Age society to achieve great public works. The eventual vitrification of hillforts such as Tap o' Noth need not however be the result of a Bruce-style spoilation, but rather a perverse desire to impress one's neighbours with a spectacular pyrotechnic display. Although a succession of outer ramparts and ditches often accompanies such hillforts, it is highly unlikely that sufficient bodies could be mustered to effectively defend such lengthy wall circumferences. They thus represent an effort to display status and impress one's neighbours. The compact Dark Age citadel-forts such as Dundurn and Dunadd and our probable North East equivalent of the Mither Tap, Bennachie, reverted to the combination of height and thickness of wall, defensible entrance and compactness, which was to be the hallmark of the early medieval castle.

The Vikings proved the effectiveness of mobile sea power in Atlantic Europe – comprehensively breaking up the land-based empire of Charlemagne, despite his professional army and elaborate fortifications. The Vikings were without doubt the success-story of Dark Age Scotland, settling most of Northern and Western Scotland by 900 AD. Although spasmodic raiding took place along the coast of North East Scotland, this Pictish heartland withstood the onslaught. It is likely that the clutch of early defended sites around the North East knuckle—Dundarg and Burghead, for example—may have been periodically occupied during this period of political uncertainty—and that these were sufficient to ward off the Scandinavian land hunger. It was through this coastal defence and the occasional shrewd marriage alliance, that the men of Pictland learnt to defend themselves against the Scandinavians, but it was the Normans, themselves Viking descendants, who were to become the masters in the art of castle building in Western Europe, eventually bringing their product into the North East by invitation—the power base for incoming warlords. The spread of the castle was closely connected with the new social order of feudalism—with its new obligation of military service. The devolution of judicial responsibility to the local level reflected the difficulties of a royal administration based far south of the Mounth.

The Normans brought into Saxon England probably the most rapid castle building programme known in history, speed being

1. Motte with a view! The Doune of Invernochty, Strathdon, former stronghold of the Earl of Mar's possessions in Donside, is the best example of a surviving Norman-style motte in North East Scotland. Its timberwork buildings and palisades long since rotted or charred by fire, it awaits the attentions of the excavator, delving carefully in the soils of its summit.

2. Hallforest Castle, Kintore, is an early 14th century rectangular tower comprising five levels, with entry at first floor level. Built of field clearance boulders and pinnings with a minimum of fuss for Sir Robert de Keith, Great Marischal of Scotland, it combines a passive ability to withstand the sudden attack with a minimum of expenditure and a modicum of domestic comfort.

3. The vaulting at Hallforest, exposed by a partial collapse of the external walling, was almost certainly constructed on temporary timber arching, possibly strengthened by beaten earth, subsequently quarried out. This made the tower house virtually fireproof, although creating considerable thrust on the external walls. The sockets for timber beams can still be seen in the internal walls.

4. Drum tower house is rectangular in ground plan, but relieved in its elegant simplicity by rounded corners and corbelled wallhead, the latter device enabling defenders to keep an eye on their wall base, and, if necessary, rain missiles on unwelcome visitors.

all-important because their conquest necessitated the secure settlement of a comparatively small feudal military elite in potentially hostile territory. The motte castle was readily constucted of timber on a natural gravel mound, protected by palisades and moat, as is vividly displayed on Queen Matilda's Bayeux Tapestry. This *DIY* castle neatly brought together the elements of ditch, bank, palisade and tower in a single package. The introduction of feudalism into Scotland was principally the work of the Scottish Canmore Kings, notably David I, who spent forty years in the English Norman Court. His successors Malcolm, William the Lion, and Alexander II and III, all shared his enthusiasm for Anglo-Norman institutions because they suited these difficult times when North Britain moved from a Dark Age tribal society with emphasis on kin relationships to a feudal system based on territorial units unrelated to kinship. With feudalism, all land was ultimately royal land. The land grants to barons involved the devolution of responsibility to the man on the motte. For example, the Burnetts of Leys, coming initially as Anglo-Saxon *Burnards* via the Lothians, became the kings' delegates in most local matters of local government. To do so effectively, they were bound to erect a castle, and in return for the land grant, they owed the monarchy precisely stated services—armed horsemen, custodians of the king's forest. Like any successful system, feudalism was reasonably flexible in its application. The old Celtic aristocracy was brought into the system side by side with the Anglo-Norman white settlers. In Aberdeenshire, the Earls of Mar were entrusted with the custody of the land between the Dee and Don, and built castles to protect it—at Kindrochit and at Invernochty.[3] Native aristocrats often intermarried with the Norman families. The Canmores were highly efficient rulers by the standards of their times. They were by no means excessively nationalistic—such feelings were to come later—indeed a contemporary account noted that 'the fortified places and burghs of the Scottish Kingdom are known to be inhabited by the English'.[4] Mottes are particularly common in Aberdeenshire, Moray and Angus. Local examples include Pitfodels, Durris, Migvie, Midmar, Strachan, Inverurie, Duffus and Huntly.[5] Motte distribution mirrors the theoretical extent of royal authority in the 12th and 13th centuries. Some like Inverurie are associated with royal burghs, but most represent the settlement of Anglo-Norman barons on their lands. Their short period of use before desertion in favour of stone towers emphasises a role as a temporary expedient. Such wooden structures, perhaps daubed with clay or hung with hides in an attempt to protect them from fire, had a very limited future in the face of the twin demands to increase strength against attack and to provide better accommodation for household and storage. Faced with this demand, the castle migrated from the motte to stand on more stable ground where stone walls could be constructed and where there was room to expand outwards and ground bearing strength to expand upwards. Knights returning from the Crusades—now part of an international knightly society—were full of new ideas for storming castles, and so the art of seigecraft was reborn. Chain mail and the crossbow were further developments as well as the professional soldier. Military minds grappled with the problem of designing a castle which was impregnable to direct assault, yet large enough to permit the occasional foray to drive off troublesome beseigers. At the upper end of the castle spectrum, the concentric ring or courtyard castle developed in 12th and 13th century Europe, but reached the North East of Scotland only towards the end of the latter century. Massive stone curtain walls were designed to form an inner enclosure, whose outer face was punctuated by protruding towers. Where there was a succession of walls and towers, each unit could be defended at once (in tiers) or successively as the outer defences were overwhelmed. A simplified version of a single curtain wall, partly salient towers and complex gate-unit is exemplified by Kildrummy Castle in Strathdon, eventually to serve as replacement for the Doune of Invernochty. The initial Norman idea of the single dominant tower implicit in the motte was retained in the massive donjon (Kildrummy's Snow Tower) but supplemented by a series of salient towers which enabled the approaches to the wall base to be swept by crossbow fire. The great hall, food store, kitchens and stables lay within the inner enclosure, with the domestic buildings occupying the position of greatest natural strength facing the deep valley known as the Back Den. A protruding chapel gable—a major weak point in the outer defences—was the subject of one of a number of changes planned for Kildrummy by Edward I in 1296, not all of which were completed. The base of a quarter tower was begun to face the chapel gable, and Kildrummy was provided with a sophisticated

5. In contrast to tower houses, Kildrummy Castle occupies a hilltop position, backed and fronted by dens—meltwater channels etched deeply into the local sandstone of which the castle is built. Additional strength is provided by a dry ditch of uncertain origins whose chronological relationships to the Edwardian courtyard and curtain wall castle remains a matter for debate.

6. The internal courtyard and salient towers of Kildrummy combine ample space for mustering and sheltering a large garrison recruited locally in times of need with the ability to defend each tower as a separate unit, against the enemy within or without the confines of the castle—or indeed against those inside whom one believed (wrongly) to be allies.

(b) The all-important latrine shoot exits on Kildrummy's western curtain wall.

7 (a) Salient tower and curtain wall at Kildrummy—the basics of the courtyard castle.

gatehouse highly reminiscent of the Edwardian castle of Harlech in North Wales.

In its scale and concept within the North East of Scotland, Kildrummy should be seen as a royal castle, part of a strategic network designed to infeudate and overawe the recalcitrant province of Moray. While an invading army could easily bypass such a castle, it would do so at its peril in that Kildrummy's large garrison, swollen by levies from the surrounding countryside in times of difficulty, could easily sally forth and creat major problems in the supply lines of the advancing army. In times of peace Kildrummy formed a secure and imposing base from which law and authority could be exercised, and was large enough to entertain the royal progresses favoured by Scottish kings in the medieval period. It contained a large open plan hall ideal for ceremonial occasions and 'bellycheer', but with a minimum of privacy for the baron and his family. When completed, Kildrummy was already an out-dated concept in the Scottish castellated scene. Attention was subsequently to concentrate on the development of what became classed as the tower house, reflecting the leanness of the Scottish purse following the Independence Wars, and the new royal policy, particularly favoured by Robert the Bruce, of devastating large castles which could prove troublesome if captured by an invading army.

The towerhouses which began to spring up throughout the North East of Scotland from the 14th century onwards were to prove an extremely long-lived concept in vertical living, in fact surviving right through to the middle of the 17th century. The towerhouse initially took the form of a standard model consisting of superimposed stone cells carried on barrel vaults set within a

---

facing page
8. Dunnottar occupies a likely Dark Age site, but its surviving stone walls relate to the presence here of the Keiths, Great Marischals of Scotland, whose rise in power and wealth began with the successful charge of the Scottish cavalry at Bannockburn. The L-plan four storey tower house with vaulted base in the foreground is early 15th century, and the site defences are strengthened by an elaborate gatehouse defended by tiers of splayed gunloops and portcullis, guaranteed to deter even the most intrepid of direct assaults. However the rooms with a view are those of the late 16th century domestic additions on the seaward side of the rock, principally the product of scholar, entrepreneur and founder of Marischal College, Aberdeen, George Keith, 5th Earl Marischal, whose town house on the Castlegate gave both name (and garden) to Marischal Street.

square or rectangular tower. At Hallforest, the accommodation is based on three such superimposed cells, each strongly barrel-vaulted with entrance at first floor level. The barrel vaults were almost certainly constructed by using a mobile timber arch framework supported on stone scarcements protruding from the wall.[6] Windows are typically restricted to narrow slits at the lower levels, and walls are extremely thick to counteract the outward thrust created by the stone vaulting. Materials are almost exclusively local in origin. Hallforest's primitive simplicity suggests a concern for the immediate future and nil flamboyance, although the slightly overhanging and parapeted wall face of the Tower of Drum indicates a token concern with appearance and active defence. Otherwise such early towers relied for their security on passive resistance within thick walls. They recall the closed-up inward looking appearances of the best of the surviving prehistoric Scottish brochs. Perhaps these early North East tower house prototypes reflect a partial breakdown of lordly jurisdiction consequent on the Independence Wars and the conflict over the Scottish Succession, and should be interpreted as the laird installed relatively securely on his estate with a minimum of outlay. These early towers should be viewed as the defensible homes of local gentry built to cope with the sudden raid rather than the formal seige. The lean lofty tower house offered one room per level, sometimes with intramural stair, but frequently access from kitchen to hall and solar involved the medieval equivalent of a Ramsay Ladder. The main defence would be from the wallhead by dropping missiles of various origins. It is likely that some towers were surrounded by barmekins, with internal outhouses and where animals could be impounded as and when necessary.[7] Some towers, like Corgarff, were provided with exit points perhaps for pouring boiling water sited immediately above the doorway which was the weakest point in such tower houses. The domestic arrangements were simple, austere and extremely primitive.

By the end of the fourteenth century and on into the fifteenth century, changes in tower house form were introduced to provide more ample accommodation of a more private nature for the family, without reducing the basic strength of the building. This was achieved in the first instance by simply adding another tower in the form of a wing, thus providing the possibility of two rooms at

9. The desire to display one's wealth, and indeed one's matrimonial status, is well displayed on the frontage of Huntly Castle. While its basic Z-plan shape permitted a range of accommodation, both private and public, and thus brought an end to the open plan living characteristic of medieval castles, nonetheless life in the castle still necessitated much negotiation of stairways. Ample fenestration, however, made domestic circumstances less trying for its occupants.

10. Glenbuchat Castle sits high above the junction of the Buchat with the Don.
Its standard Z-plan format includes at least one architectural quirk—a pair of
large semi-inserted stair turrets sitting on arches (trompes) rather than on the
more conventional corbels—the former being an architectural tradition with a
French connection. The marriage of Glenbuchat's first owner, John Gordon to
Helen Carnegie, proudly displayed above the door, may be the connection. Helen
was the daughter of the Scottish ambassador at Henry II of France's court,
present at the time when the influential French architect Philibert de l'Orme,
whose work included part of the Tuileries, published his *magnus opus* on
architecture, within which trompes featured. Note the use of sandstone for the
label corbelling of the square angle turret—possibly carved by a mason imported
from Helen Carnegie's Angus homeland. (Print from Billings.)

11. Knock Castle, by Ballater, is a sturdy oblong tower house with angle turret supported by label corbelling, four storeys high, and designed for defence by, and against, small arms. As with most of its contemporaries, the house was surrounded by a small courtyard (barmekin), containing domestic offices, possibly even the kitchen facilities. Knock was traditionally a Gordon stronghold, and may well have been rebuilt, or at least modified to its present form, at the beginning of the 17th century.

12. The Jacobean courtyard mansion house of Drum (from 1619) was tacked onto William de Irwin's early 14th century tower. The mansion displays the increasing attention to external and internal architecture appropriate to its period. The open and welcoming aspect of the building is a very striking feature.

each level (The L-plan tower house). There was improved access to the higher floors provided by the insertion of intramural or spiral staircases. The increased control of the ground surrounding the castle by firearms discharged via basal shot loops, and the almost ubiquitous use of the yett permitted the doorway to descend to ground level, relatively securely positioned in the re-entrant angle between the two towers or wings. A variety of angle turrets were provided above, increasing the field of fire by downward slanting shot loops. Similar improvements were incorporated into the prototype rectangular tower houses which were still proving popular. At Knock on the Royal Estate of Birkhall, a small rectangular tower house with vaulted ground floor includes a newel stairway close to the entrance and a private stair from the hall on the first floor to the cellar. Each of the windows is provided with three shot loops under the sill, set diagonally to command all directions of approach, and there are also shot holes in the corner turrets. Here in a house measuring only 7m by 9m, walls remain over one metre thick.

In the fifteenth century, while castles were still required, their layout and external appearance evolved in response to continued social change with a desire for more light and space, increased domestic comfort and privacy and the aim of impressing not only one's enemies but also one's friends. There followed a growing and infectious desire for decorative detail in the exterior, perhaps paralleling the rather ostentatious nature of 16th century dress. Fireplaces are extremely decorative as are the heraldic insignia which sprout everywhere, both inside and out. Those doughty men who built the new breed of castles in the North East were both master masons *and* architects. From the 1480s to the Scottish Reformation in the 1560s, few new tower houses were built, perhaps reflecting the long term effect of defeat of the Scottish chivalry at Flodden. Thereafter construction began anew with the cessation of widespread baronial conflict. The traditional style of tower house expanded in new directions, fuelled by the sequestration of church land, the revenues of estates and the development of widespread trading links with the continent. The European Renaissance brought in new influences in architectural detail and interior decoration. The concept of vertical living was retained but planned with growing imagination and skill. Subtle improvements in defensive potential were incorporated with increasing

room at the top. Access to the upper levels at Corse is provided by
a stair placed diagonally opposite from the entrance doorway via a
single salient tower built specifically to facilitate access to the
upper levels. The Aberdeenshire Z-plan castle, basically three
towers slapped together, as at Harthill, Terpersie and Castle
Fraser reflects variations on a common theme—increasing
domesticity within a secure defensive framework but with varying
imputs of resources. At Castle Fraser and Craigievar, the austere
lower courses are surmounted by exuberant even flamboyant
details at the upper levels, the protruding turrets in the latter case
compensating for the loss of floor space caused by the inward
sloping walls. The laird's hall with musical gallery, elaborately
panelled and with on occasion, as at Muchalls and Craigievar,
heraldic carved ceilings in plaster, all reflect a laird who has
become a civilised person, perhaps with a degree from the
university, owner of a productive estate, and a member of the
mercantile class. These new defensive houses are set in pleasant
surroundings with little care for the strategic control of ground,
rather a southerly aspect and rooms with a view. The continued
addiction to height as opposed to breadth may represent the
difficulty of obtaining large timber beams as much as the
maintenance of the tower tradition. The most elaborate of the
castles of this period are almost chateau-like in appearance, as
well displayed at Fyvie and Castle Fraser. Here, as elsewhere,
there was much use of the ornate corbelling and grotesque
gargoyles, some of the latter in the form of imitation cannon. The
castle of Leslie on the Gadie is one of the last of the North-East's
tower houses—its profusion of gun and pistol loops are combined
internally with an open stairway with ample landings, suggesting
that perhaps the only form of potential aggression envisaged here
was domestic in origin! By the middle of the 17th century when
Leslie was built, the county house was the laird's desirable
residence of the future, and the days of the castle as a fortress or
defensive home had long since run their course.

Conclusion

Castles developed as the tangible response of a society under
pressure from invasion and social change, forcing together the
elements of home and fortress. It seems possible that Viking

13. The genius of Bel displayed at Craigievar. Vertical living in the grand style.

14. The upper echelons of Craigievar bristle with exuberant gargoyles and emblems associated with the desire of the Forbes's to display their mercantile wealth for all to see. The castle sits on open ground with a southerly aspect, and reaches high, perhaps as much a result of scarcity of quality timber for beams (despite Danzig Willie's Baltic connections) as a traditional means of defence.

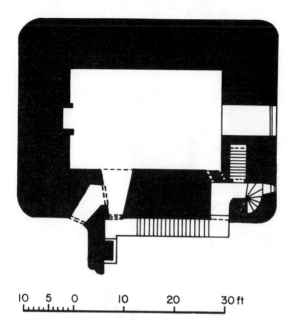

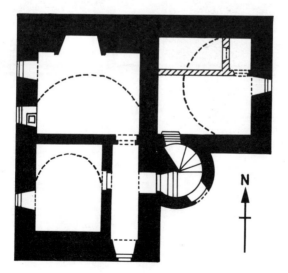

15. Upper: plan of first floor at Drum tower.
Lower: plan of ground floor at Braemar.

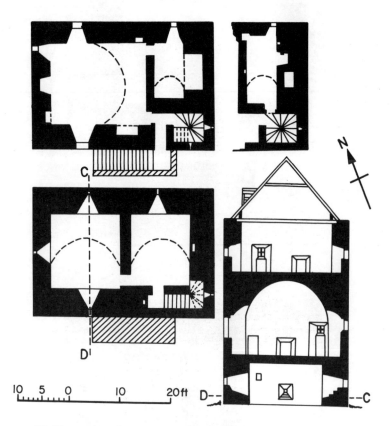

16. Plan and section of Corgarff Castle as originally constructed
(after W. D. Simpson).

17. The small rectangular tower house of Corgarff, remote and sitting at over 1400 feet above sea level, was constructed in its original form in the 16th century for the Forbes as a hunting seat. It also served as a place with defensive potential, sitting as it did astride the raiding routes between Speyside and Strathdon. Although burnt in the infamous Edom O' Gordon episode, its internal vaulting permitted survival in viable form for restoration and substantial internal modification after 1745 for the accommodation of Hanoverian troops.

raiding activities stimulated the construction of the North East's first castles, although it was the Anglo-Normans, themselves descendents of the Vikings, who introduced castle building on a wide scale. Their motte and bailey castles were the power base for controlling territory and were the tangible face of feudalism. The art of fortification was learnt through bitter experience both at home and abroad e.g. The Crusades. The large courtyard castles like Kildrummy (and possibly Fyvie in its original form?)—scarcely reached the North East, but displayed the thinking of the professional military minds who sought to devise a castle which was impregnable to direct assault by conventional means, yet large enough to permit a sally by the large garrison to drive off attackers or break and supply lines. Already the professional soldier particularly the crossbow man, was a feature of significance in castle design. For much of the *floruit* of such castles, ceremony and the collection of rent in kind were the normal duties of its tenant or owner. On the basis that one cannot always trust one's friends, let alone one's enemies, castles like Kildrummy consisted of independently defensible parts. Living was largely open plan with the minimum of privacy and comfort. Early stone tower houses were stark and primitive, with much vaulting, perhaps built by masons who worked on churches as well as castles—the only stone buildings in a landscape of wood and wattle structures.

With more peaceful times, the castle increasingly became a defensible residence, built with an eye for increased domestic comfort. Formal seigeworks were always the exception in remote North East Scotland, so tower houses were designed to withstand the sudden raid with handweapons, fire and small arms. Specialist masons emerged to capture the market in tower design, stimulated by the requirements of mercantile lairds who desired to combine comfort and security with a public display of success in their home. Vertical living continued but relieved by subtle innovations in internal design and access between floors. By the end of the 16th century when the tower house has reached the end of its course, these buildings stood in open ground amid pleasant surroundings, with their relatively warlike silhouettes contradicting the peaceful aspirations of their owners.

REFERENCES

1. *Chambers twentieth century dictionary*—revised edition, 1959.
2. J.W. Hedges and B. Bell, 'That tower of prehistory—the broch', *Antiquity*, 54, 1980, 93.
3. The topography on which the 17th century Braemar Castle sits and its site adjacent to the ancient kirk of St Andrew strongly suggests a motte-style castle may have stood there prior to the construction of the phase one stone-built Kindrochit Castle.
4. W. Croft Dickinson, *Scotland from earliest times to 1603*. Revised and edited by A.A.M. Duncan, third edition, Oxford, 1977, 106.
5. P.A. Yeoman, 'Excavations at Castlehill of Strachan 1980–81', *Proceedings of the Society of Antiquaries of Scotland*, 114, 1984, 315–64.
6. I am indebted to Professor James Gibson, Boat of Garten, a participant in the conference, who drew my attention to this method of vault construction, as displayed in the 12th century Cistercian Abbey of Senangue, Gordes-Vaucluse, Central France. Sister houses of Cistercian houses were of course founded in Scotland under the aegis of David I.
7. C.J. Tabraham, 'The Scottish medieval towerhouse as lordly residence in the light of recent excavations', *Proceedings of the Society of Antiquaries of Scotland*, 118, 1988, 267–77.

PARKS, GARDENS AND POLICIES: THE CHANGING LANDSCAPE AROUND THE CASTLE

T.R. Slater

The immediate surroundings of castles of North East Scotland enjoyed many of the attributes long recognised in castles in the Lowlands. They included elements such as gardens, orchards, dovecotes, rabbit warrens and woodland enclosures in their immediate vicinity. The most extensive, and amongst the earliest, of these landscape elements was the medieval deer park. Gilbert's researches into the deer parks of medieval Scotland[1] have clearly established that Anglo-Norman influences had introduced the deer park into the country by the thirteenth century. Quite a large number of these parks can be documented, notably on royal estates and on the lands of the principal feudal lords, but whether the use to which they were put was equivalent to those on English estates is more difficult to establish. They could enclose anything from fifty to several thousand acres with an embankment, ditch, and a wooden pale fence or wall and contained a deer herd which, when nourished through the winter months, provided both a ready source of meat and captive animals which could be released for the pleasures of the hunt in the wider forest or moorland.

With its extensive mountains and moorland areas it is perhaps not surprising that the North East records relatively few of these special enclosures. Most were along the Highland margins of Perthshire and in the valleys of the Dee, Don and Spey. However, the region does contain what Gilbert suggests is the best-preserved medieval park pale bank surviving in the Scottish countryside: to the north of Kincardine castle.[2] Kincardine park was probably created by William I and was enlarged by Alexander III in 1266. Red and fallow deer were the main game animals, but swans and boar were other animals protected in parks.

Parks continued to be made into the seventeenth century and, since in the medieval period deer parks were virtually the only enclosures to be found in the countryside, 'park' became the generic term in Scotland for any walled or hedged enclosure used for pasturing livestock.[3] Such enclosures became the concern of government in the sixteenth century. A number of orders were made to encourage landowners to 'mak them to have parkis with dere and plant at the leist ane aker of wood'.[4] The second part of this regulation betokens the concern for the lack of timber resources in the country and it is clearly from the sixteenth century that lairds began to enclose small areas on their estates for tree plantations as well as pasture. Both activities demonstrate a concern for both the practicalities of living in castles (food, fuel and building materials), and with estate improvement in terms of increased rents.

Whether many of the castles of the North East had gardens and orchards in the medieval period is open to doubt. Certainly, elsewhere in Scotland, there is both historical and archaeological evidence for small, late-medieval terrace gardens for herbs and flowers adjoining even quite small castles,[5] and for orchards, normally enclosed with walls, in the vicinity. They would have supplied the household with fruit and vegetables and it seems probable that at least the more prominent castles of the North East region might have had such gardens and orchards, though none are documented that I am aware of.

The enforcement of government regulations for parks and plantations was no doubt difficult in the remoter corners of the North East but it is clear from the evidence of the maps in the Blaeu atlas that, by the first half of the seventeenth century, such emparking and planting had taken place on a quite extensive scale.[6] The parks at Gordon Castle are particularly prominent on the map of Morayshire, for example. This particular landscape probably dates from the 1630s when the Marquis of Huntly is said to 'give himself whollie to policie, planting and building';[7] certainly the much-enlarged castle was constructed at this time. A decade earlier we find Sir Robert Gordon urging the youthful Earl of Sutherland 'to build a house in Dunrobin for that is the . . . most pleasant habitation you hawe. Ther yow may easilie mak a fyne delicat park'.[8] A few years later the Earl's efforts are described in one of the most detailed evocations of an early

seventeenth-century garden which we have for the castles of the
North East:

> Dunrobin, The Earl of Sutherland's special residence, a house well
> seated upon a motte, hard by the sea, with fair orchards where there
> be pleasant gardens planted with all kinds of froots, hearbs and
> floors used in this kingdom; and abundance of good saffron, tobacco
> and rosemary. The froot here is excellent and chiefly the pears and
> cherries . . . One mile from the castle there is a fair coneygar, three
> miles in length along the sea coast, very well stored and full of
> coneys.[9]

Coneys are, of course, rabbits.

Such development is known to have been comparatively
common further south but clearly, even in the remote fastness of
Sutherland, let alone in the Moray Firth lowlands and Aberdeenshire, at least the larger castles had gardens, orchards, deer park
and rabbit warren by the mid seventeenth century. Meals for the
castle household might have arrived lukewarm for consumption,
after the long treck from kitchen to hall, but at least they seem to
have been constituted from varied and nutritious ingredients
grown on the estate. The reference to saffron and tobacco suggests
that the Earl of Sutherland was experimenting with new crops in
his gardens, the latter perhaps as a result of a gift from the king.
The mention of the excellence of the fruit is not at all untypical.
Scottish monasteries, in particular, seem to have developed good
varieties of apples, pears and cherries suited to the Scottish
climate and many of these varieties were taken into the newly-
made orchards of the lairds soon after the Dissolution.[10] In some
instances, of course, a laird's tower house superceded a monastic
institution directly and orchards and gardens could be taken over
as working concerns.

Another contemporary description of a garden in the North
East is that written to record the destruction of the gardens of
Banff Castle in 1640 as the Civil War raged. Sir George Ogilvie's
estate on the edge of the town was occupied by General Munro:

> Who no sooner came thither, but he sett downe his qwarter in the
> laird of Banfe his beautiful garden, which was a great ornament to
> the towne of Banfe, and, being gallantly planted and walled,
> overshadowd and enclosd the east syde of that towne. The

souldiours wer no sooner sett downe there but they fell to macke havocke of all the standing trees, younge nor old, and cutting upp all the hedges to the rootes; in which deformed condition it is yet to be seen as they left it.[11]

Another account describes the garden as 'inclosed with excellent stone-walls, and planted with the best fruit-trees then could be had'.[12] Ogilvie was one of those lairds who favoured the King and he had not only fine gardens but a castle which he had extended and on which he had lavished much expenditure. It, too, was left an uninhabitable shell by the troops.

From the Restoration to the '45

The Restoration of Charles II in 1660 provoked the next clear stimulus to change for two reasons: first, the Court had been resident in France for more than a decade and had absorbed many of the cultural precepts of that nation during their exile, including its innovative garden styles; and, secondly, from 1660 more Scottish aristocrats made the long journey south to London on a regular basis to attend on the king. On these journeys, and while in the capital, they were open to the influence of English ways of estate management,[13] English garden styles, the new plant materials being brought in from the expanding colonies, and the ever-changing kaleidoscope of fashion in everything from architecture to clothing.[14] As a result many Scottish lords began to refurbish their castles to make them more comfortable for daily living, or even to completely replace them with new mansions.[15] With this rebuilding of the residence went a hand-in-hand refashioning of the landscape around the castles.

Some of these new layouts were both spectacular in design and on an enormous scale. This was particularly so in Perthshire where, for example, the Earl of Strathmore's castle at Glamis, re-edified in 1679–83, continued to impress visitors and travellers for the next half century. Robert Sibbald described the new gardens just as they were being created as:

a great and excellent hous newly re-edified and furnished most stately with everything necessare, with excellent gaites, avenues, courts, gairdin, bouling-greens, parks, enclosures, hay meadowes and planting; very beautifull and pleasant . . . There is a cuningare within the park and dovecoat at the burn.[16]

There was also one of the great stone sundials (Fig.18) which are such a distinctive feature of Scottish seventeenth-century gardens.[17] It is described by Lord Strathmore:

> Ther is in the gardin a fine dyal erected and how soon the walk and green plots are layed there will be statu's put into it, and there is a designe for a fountain in the bouling green.[18]

The famous statue garden was described in great detail after its completion by John Macky in the 1720s. The palace:

> stands in the middle of a well-planted park, with avenues cut through every way to the house. The great avenue, thickly planted on each side, at the entrance of which is the great stone gate, . . . leads you in half a mile to the outer court, which has a statue on each side of the top of the gate as big as the life. On the great gate of the inner court are ballustrades of stone, finely adorn'd with statues and in the court are four brazen statues, bigger then the life, on pedestals. . . . From this court, by ballustrades of iron, you have a full prospect of the gardens on each side, cut out into grass-plats, and adorn'd with ever-greens, which are very well kept.[19]

Sibbald's description provides three distinct emphases which are important in understanding the nature of castle surroundings at this time. First, there is a concern with improved estate economy—parks (i.e. pasture closes), enclosures, hay meadows, rabbit warren and dovecot. Lairds were in the forefront of agricultural improvement in the later seventeenth century. Improved agriculture went hand-in-hand with better pastures, enclosures, shelter belts of woodland and better administration, and this improvement in the economy of the estate began with the home farms of the laird himself. Secondly, there is a recognition of recreation; the bowling green in particular was a fashionable attribute being added to many gardens at this time where the gentlemen could amuse themselves, though hunting continued to be popular. Thirdly, there is the increasingly formal design of the lands around the castle—avenues, courts and tree planting in geometric patterns.

This new formality in the design of the surroundings of castles came from France, both directly, and as it had been adapted by English gardeners and lords. The direct French influence is seen

18. The great stone sun-dial at Glamis Castle (Forfarshire) erected by Patrick,
11th Earl of Mar, as illustrated by Macgibbon and Ross in their survey of Scottish
castles (1887).

most clearly in the planting of woodlands. Scottish planting tended to be of solid, geometric blocks of trees divided by broad rides with occasional classical statues or buildings providing eye-catchers at rond points within the design. In England, avenues of trees with grassland tended to be preferred. The other feature of the late seventeenth and early eighteenth centuries which also very much derived from the continent was the provision of grand parterres with canals and fountains and formalised, grass-covered terraces. John Reid's first Scottish gardening book took up this new fashion and helped to spread the ideas by decreeing that:

> all the buildings and plantings should ly so about the house as that the house may be at the centre, all the walks, trees and hedges running to the house. Therefore whatever you have on the one hand make as much of the same form and in the same place on the other.[20]

In other words, in designing gardens, balance and complementarity were all important in the success of the layout from the late seventeenth century onwards.

Grand parterres were the province of the greater landowners of course; the majority of lairds followed the older tradition of small enclosed gardens around the castle, though they were certainly laid out more formally as Reid had recommended. For illustration of this period we can turn to William Adam's grand design of c.1720 at Taymouth in Perthshire for the Earl of Breadalbane.[21] The intricate regular gardens were extended into the countryside by great avenues of triple lines of trees in the characteristic Anglo-French *patte d'oi*, or goose-foot, pattern (Fig.19). However, there was also the first glimmering of a new fashion favouring the irregular and natural in the sinuous walk laid out alongside the meanders of the river. A description of Tyrie (Aberdeenshire) in 1723, notes a similar parkland and garden planned in the 1690s with:

> Large orchards and arming of barren planting (i.e. a goosefoot) and at foot of the parks, below the house eastward, is a pretty cannal or water draught of 12 foot broad, near a mile in length.[22]

There were also, '3 handsome terraces' on each side of the river at nearby Boyndlie with, 'a pair of stairs ascending by 12 steps to the hous from a handsome avenue and square from the utter gate'. The house was 'invironed with fyne gardens well-planted and

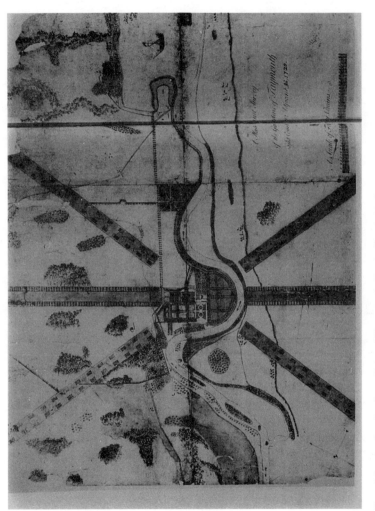

19. William Adam's plan for the policies of Taymouth Castle (Perthshire) of 1720. Reproduced from A. A. Tait (1980).

walled with rounds on every corner . . . with a summer hous and
ducat'.[23] However, Macky, rather unfairly, considered that,
despite such estates, in Aberdeenshire there was 'neither fine
architecture nor gardening in the large shire, but abundance of
good cheer and good neighbourhood'.[24]

One of the best descriptions of an estate at the turn of the
eighteenth century refers to Urie Castle near Stonehaven, then the
home of the Barclays. There:

> the house is an old castle-built house having very thick strong walls.
> . . . The gardens are very delightfully placed below one another quite
> to the riverside . . . The present owner . . . hath planted a great many
> trees of several sorts, particularly fir trees, which thrive very well, he
> is supposed to have near an hundred thousand. . . . One remarkable
> curiosity of planting made by him is not to be omitted, viz. upon the
> north end of his cherry garden and in view of his windows, he hath
> planted a piece of ground equall in breadth to his garden, the rowes
> and openings answering every side, with twentie five different sorts
> of barren trees, and so exactly regular, that where there is one or
> more of one sorts of trees . . . it hath the same in the opposite side,
> which with the different colours of the leaves so nicely intermixed
> and variety of foliage, makes a charming show, he hath made . . . a
> very beautifull pond, with two islands in it, planted with trees, in
> which the wild ducks breed . . . and the rising ground round it
> planted with trees of severall sorts as elms, birch and fir, and willows
> near the water.[25]

It is noteworthy that 'barren trees', that is non fruit trees, could
still be thought so unusual in the early eighteenth century. Many
other landowners were also experimenting with conifers newly
imported from the American colonies. Pococke describes the
Wilderness at Blair Atholl (Perthshire) (Fig.20) as:

> A vale, which is most beautifully planted with many sorts of
> American trees; this is called Diana's Grove, from a statue of her
> with a stag on rising ground, from which there are eight walks. . . . In
> this grove there is a walk of tall larch trees cut up within like a
> hedge.[26]

Blair Atholl was famed for its larch plantations, established by the
2nd Duke from 1737.[27]

One of the most important garden designers of this period was
Thomas Winter. A surveyor turned gardener, he worked for Sir

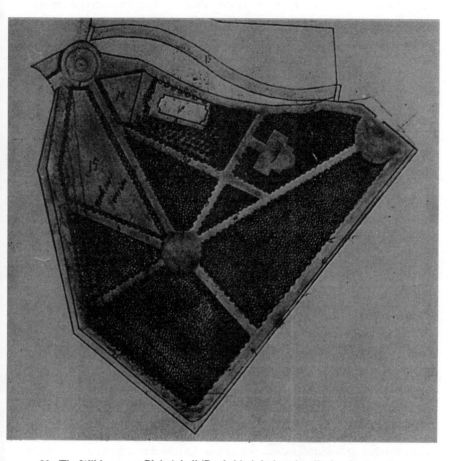

20. The Wilderness at Blair Atholl (Perthshire) designed to display the American and other conifers grown by James, 2nd Duke of Atholl. (Photo R.C.A.H.M.S.)

Archibald Grant on his well-known estate improvements at Monymusk (Aberdeenshire) from 1726.[28] The latter is described by Bishop Pococke in 1760 as:

> a very great improver in the farm and garden. . . . He has made a fine plantation; first you come into an orchard, then to an avenue of firrs with parterres on each side: there is also a pleasant walk by the river; and the hills to the south are covered with trees.[29]

Winter began to branch out on his own when he designed a layout for the Glamis estate in 1746. This respected earlier elements in the layout, as did the neat formal garden for Sir James Grant at Castle Grant (Morayshire), which he designed in 1748.[30] His designs were conservative when compared with stylistic advances being made in England, and even in parts of the Lowlands. Winter was wary of the new taste and was aware of its unsuitability for the upland landscapes framing many of the estates in the North East. North-East landowners, too, were more concerned with the practicalities of vegetable and fruit growing rather than with fashionable design and Winter was prepared to give them what they wanted. Elegance and fashion are only possible once the necessities of life have been provided and, in the North East, most lairds were still more concerned with improving their estates economically.

Another example of this conservatism, even on a large estate, is, again, Blair Atholl where a plan of 1751 shows an old-fashioned kitchen garden with garden houses, dovecote, and brick walls for the growing of espalier fruit trees and the shelter of more delicate plants similar to that described at Urie castle earlier. The policies, too, at Blair in the mid eighteenth century were still divided by formal, tree-lined rides with characteristic French-style roundels at the intersections, the individual parks being used for pasture or, in this case, for wilderness trees and the famous larches.[31, 32]

Plans become an important source of evidence from the mid eighteenth century for many estates. For instance, there are no good descriptions of the formal gardens at Gordon Castle (Morayshire), but a series of fine estate plans enable their form to be reconstructed.[33] Again, there were grass terraces, statues, a canal, fountains, bowling greens and orchards, together with the park, which contained a dovecot, and enclosures for horses, cattle and swans (Fig.21). There is also the first hint, as at Taymouth, of

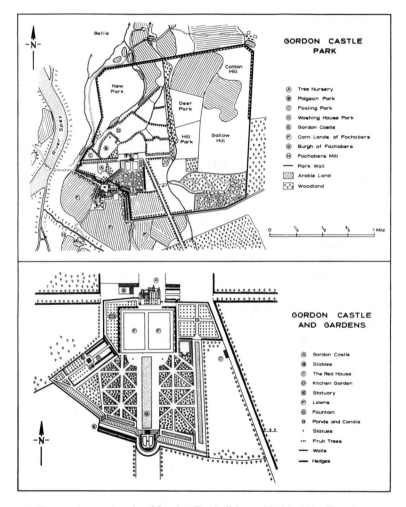

21. The gardens and parks of Gordon Castle (Morayshire) in 1764. The plans are
derived from the Gordon Castle MSS. Scottish Record Office R.H.P, 2312, 2379.

the new mid eighteenth century ideas on informality with winding paths laid out in the quarry woodland garden to the east of the castle. None of this is more than hinted at in written descriptions which talk only of 'large gardens, orchards, plantings, entries and parks',[34] or of 'fine gardens and a very spacious deer park'.[35] The likelihood is that the Duke of Gordon did not encourage casual visitors on to his estates.

These estates which peppered the Highland straths and the coastal lowlands of the North East were, of course, islands of enclosure and planting in a sea of open runrig lands and muirs and mosses as Roy's map of the mid eighteenth century well illustrates (British Museum Maps C9b). In the Highlands, places such as Invercauld and Braemar were spectacular islands of plantation and designed regularity in a wild, open landscape (Fig.22). And things were little different in the lowlands. The castles and houses of aristocrat and laird, with their little enclosures of field pasture and plantation, stand out clearly from the generality of the open countryside from Perthshire in the south, up through Aberdeen-shire, and westwards along the Moray coastlands. Roy's map demonstrates more clearly than anything, that the enclosure of the countryside and the capitalisation of agriculture began on the mains farms of the laird and the great landowner.

The Beautiful and the Picturesque

The next stimulus to change was the aftermath of the '45. Many estates changed hands; whilst other lairds removed themselves quietly from the political scene and began to look to the improvement of their estates. By the 1760s, runrig lands were being enclosed, water-powered mills were being established, villages rebuilt and replanned, and extensive plantations began to be established around policies and on steeper slopes. Newly landscaped policies in the informal style which followed the ideals of 'the Beautiful', popularised in England by 'Capability' Brown, began to be made in Scotland, and some English gardeners established practices which extended into Scotland. Robert Robinson, for example, like Winter before him, built up contacts through Sir Archibald Grant at Monymusk. He served an apprenticeship with Brown but then set up on his own in Scotland. He provided an extensive plan for Sir James Grant for the policies

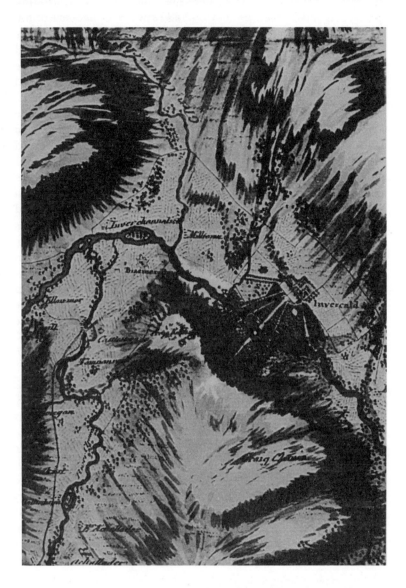

22. The Invercauld area (Aberdeenshire) from Roy's Military Survey of Scotland (1747–55). Copyright, British Library.

of Castle Grant in 1764, with sinuous belts of trees, curving drives, naturalistic lakes, clumps, and broad lawns up to the house, and with the kitchen garden banished far from the house. He also worked at Banff and Glamis in the same year, and at Cullen House in 1766.[36]

The Scottish upland landscape was far more suited to the ideals of the Picturesque than to the Beautiful, and those designers who tried to reproduce English landscape gardens in Scotland usually failed miserably in the eyes of contemporary opinion. Even landowners were aware of these shortcomings and, for example, when Robinson provided a design for the refashioning of the landscape of Glamis castle, which would have swept away the magnificent formal garden to replace it with lawns and clumps and belts, it was not used. Rather, James Abercrombie was commissioned to provide another design four years later, and though this, too, was for a landscape garden, Abercrombie was anxious to preserve the most venerable elements of the earlier, formal design, including the great main avenue and the gate before the castle. The old gardens were only finally levelled in 1775.[37]

Picturesque sensibilities looked to use rushing water rather than still ponds; enjoyed the crags of incised burns and irregular planting, and of ancient buildings and romantic ruins—even if they had to be new-built! James Bowie's Gothic tower beside Alvah bridge, which gave access to Duff House at Banff, was much admired for its picturesqueness,[38] but the landscape to which it gave access around the house was much more designed in the mode of the Beautiful. The Earl of Findlater's Cullen House, nearby, perhaps provided a model, as it, too, was perched above a wooded gorge which William Adam had bridged over in the early eighteenth century. He had provided winding walks along the valley with a wilderness of trees around the house, but the wider policies were still laid out as rectangular parks divided with avenues of fir trees when mapped by Peter May in 1764 (Fig.23).[39, 40] It is described by Pococke in 1760 as having:

> pleasant winding walks through the wood, partly in sight of the river and partly at a distance with a walk likewise over the high ground. The fields are planted, as are the hills to the west, which will appear very beautifull when the firr trees grow up.[41]

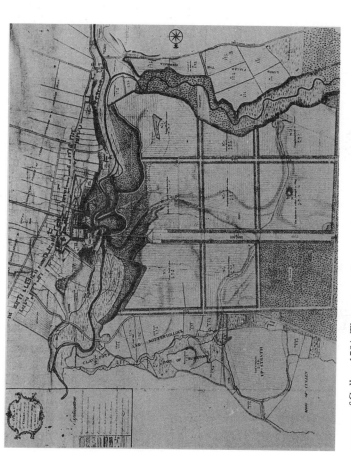

23. Peter May's survey of Cullen, 1764. The contrast between the rectangular pasture marks with their shelter belts and the irregular planting of the valley is notable. The town was to be demolished later in the early 19th century. Reproduced from A. A. Tait (1980).

One of the most significant forces in the changes in the design of policies which came about in the mid eighteenth century was a greater desire for privacy on the part of the landowners and lairds. Lord Fife, at Duff House, for example, was writing to his factor in 1765 to employ a park-keeper 'just to keep idle people from going through the park . . . nothing makes the place so disagreeable to me as that constant crowd of idle people that are walking over my grounds when I am at home',[42] while the Duchess of Gordon was noting in the same year that there were '3 or 4 strumpets in Fochabers who are notorious thieves & are become so impudent as to steal things from the washing house & to skulk frequently about the castle'.[43]

At Gordon Castle, it was again not until the late 1760s that things began to change. The driving force seems to have been not the easy-going young 4th Duke, but his forceful Duchess who was determined that everything should be to her liking. Sadly, everything that could go wrong did so, as a succession of second-rate architects and designers wrought havoc with the castle, policies and town. Fochabers had become a flourishing small market town in the first half of the eighteenth century with the encouragement of an earlier generation of Gordons[44] but, by 1770, it was, as we have seen, too close for the Duchess's liking. Nonetheless, the Duke began to improve his estates as most other landowners did, by rebuilding his great castle. A little foresight might have suggested placing it in the centre of his policies, well away from the town, but John Baxter's vast new house was finished in 1781 on the site of its castle predecessor, and partly incorporating it.[45] As the new castle was being finished the great formal gardens were razed by the Duke's head gardener and Thomas Reid, a nursery gardener from Banff. The canal was filled in in 1779 and the grass slopes of the parterre were levelled, leaving only the formal avenues of trees (Fig.24).[46] And they were not to survive for very much longer. Reid supplied shrubs to furnish the lawns and Baxter provided 'a sketch of a new town agreeable to your Grace's idea of having it square and compact' (Fig.24).[47]

Naturally, a proper landscape design was required for the policies and, in 1786, Thomas White provided a grand plan. White was an Englishman with an extensive practice in the north and in Scotland who specialised in particularly insipid landscapes,

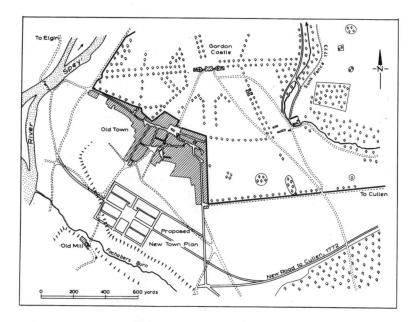

24. Fochabers c.1773. The plans for new town and new roads are superimposed on the fields of Fochabers and the formal gardens have been swept away from the policies. Derived from Scottish Records Office R.H.P. 2381, 2356.

using the elements of Brown's style, but without his verve and eye for effect,—so that is what the Duke got. White had four major commissions in the North East in the 1780s and 1790s; at Scone Palace, Gordon Castle, Cullen House and Duff House, Banff. White was a man with a reputation for taking advantage of his aristocratic employers in terms of fees and hospitality, as well as for paying little attention to his design work. There is a story recounted by Lauder that the Duke of Gordon was one of those who suffered. White, having spent several weeks at Gordon Castle during which he rarely left the comforts of the drawing room, demanded that the view to the River Spey be opened up by cutting down a fine grove of trees. A year later, again enjoying the Duke's hospitality, the friable red banks of the Spey were now in full view from the house and White advised the Duke to plant a clump of trees to hide what he thought was a brickfield! The Duke was not amused.[48]

The most spectacular feature of the new policies at Gordon Castle, which were not fully completed until 1792, was a sunk fence, or ha ha, more than 2km long which divided the lawns of the policies from the pasture lands in the parks beyond (Fig.24). The lawns and shelter belts were on an immense scale but the lake was tiny and had almost dried up within a century. The Duke was also at work beyond the policies. The town's runrig fields were enclosed in 1772, and the main road to Cullen was realigned to run around the park and through the site of the new town that Baxter had planned for him. In 1776, the Duke's solicitor began to issue feus for the new town and to buy up the old town plots. Unlike most new towns and villages in the North East there was no advertising and no encouragement of manufacturers.[49] The new village was intended as an estate village and as an edification of the policies. Baxter designed the principal buildings on the central square and provided a model design for use by cottagers elsewhere in the town.[50]

The majority of the old town feuars were unwilling to move and various means both fair and foul were used to encourage them. Removal expenses were paid but they were insufficient to cover the cost of the new houses. It was not until 1802 that the last feuar left old Fochabers and the town was finally demolished to enable White's plan for the policies to be completed.[51] The new village provided a prelude to the grand gates and broad, sweeping drive round to the castle for visitors travelling the highway from Aberdeen. Within the gates, extensive shrubberies hid the new kitchen-garden walls from view and broad lawns stretched up to the walls of the house (Fig.25). The flourishing little burgh of Fochabers had been transformed, according to Lord Cockburn, into:

> a kennel for the retired lacqueys and ladies' maids of the castle and for the natural children and pensioned mistresses of the noble family, with a due proportion of factors, gamekeepers and all the other adherents of such establishments.[52]

Fochabers witnessed enormous changes in the second half of the eighteenth century and a similar pattern of reordering the landscape can also be followed at places such as Castle Grant and Cullen House where settlements were also replanned to improve the landscape setting of the castles and houses of aristocratic

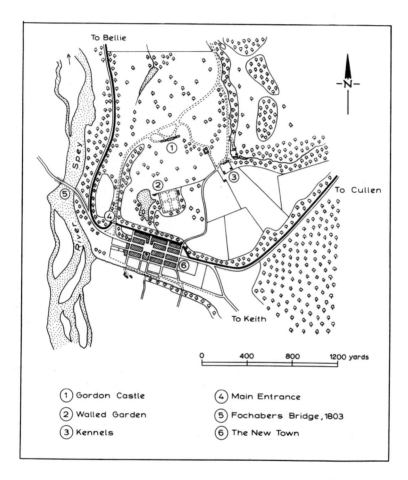

To Bellie

To Cullen

To Keith

-N-

0   400   800   1200 yards

① Gordon Castle   ④ Main Entrance

② Walled Garden   ⑤ Fochabers Bridge, 1803

③ Kennels   ⑥ The New Town

25. Fochabers c.1810. The old burgh has been demolished and the vast tree-studded lawns of the policies of Gordon Castle were secure in the privacy of their walls and plantations. Scottish Record Office R.H.P. 2386.

landowners. Grantown was replanned and rebuilt from 1766[53] and Cullen from 1822.[54] But on smaller estates it is the comparative conservatism of owners in refurbishing and redesigning their policies and gardens that marks out the North East, and indeed much of Scotland. Where money was available for investment in the residence a little remodelling, a small extension to the building, would be in order, and a little refurbishment of gardens and orchards and some new planting of trees, especially if they helped to shelter new pasture parks. But, mostly, gardens, orchards and plantations were left to mature and sometimes to decay. For this reason, once formality, flower beds and order became fashionable once more in the mid nineteenth century, older layouts needed little effort to resurrect them. The reconstruction of the great formal garden at Drummond Castle by gardeners Lewis and Kennedy in the 1820s and 1830s, centred on its fine sixteenth-century sundial, is one example of such restoration, and the famous gardens of Pitmedden another.

In the 1820s, too, descriptions were beginning to reflect this new appreciation of the old. J.C. Loudon, for example, was moved to talk of 'the excellent kitchen garden in the old style, with magnificent holly hedges, abundance of prolific fruit trees, and venerable exotic shrubs' at Crathes Castle.[55] Crathes was also described appreciatively a decade earlier by Robertson as:

> The best garden that, perhaps, I have met with in Scotland. . . . It extends over about 4 English acres, and is laid out in the ancient style of straight walks bounded by broad hedges of holly and yew which are trimmed with great precision, perpendicular in the sides and flat at the top, and so thick and strong that one might almost walk upon them. Among other ornamental shrubs I noticed here the Portugal Laurel in full blossom.

Nearby, at Brotherton,

> on the coast side, is another garden in the ancient style. This is bounded and subdivided not by hedges, but by stone walls; and is raised terrace above terrace with a strength of masonry which might serve fortification.[56]

These gardens framed either original castles and tower houses dating from the seventeenth century or earlier, or, more rarely, new-built residences in Scots Baronial style inspired by Sir Walter Scott's Abbotsford and Queen Victoria's rebuilding of Balmoral in the 1850s. With this new appreciation of formal gardens around the building, the story of parks, gardens and policies in the North East comes almost full circle but the formal gardens of the later nineteenth century were set in a wider landscape that was very different. It was an enclosed landscape of hedged or walled fields, neat villages, straight roads and extensive plantations, not a landscape of open moor and moss.

REFERENCES

1. J.M. Gilbert, *Hunting and hunting reserves in medieval Scotland* (Edinburgh, 1979).
2. Ibid., 215–18.
3. T.R. Slater, 'The mansion and policy' in M.L. Parry and T.R. Slater (eds.), *The making of the Scottish countryside* (London, 1980), 227.
4. W.C. Dickinson, G. Donaldson and I.A. Milne (eds.), *Source book of Scottish History* (Edinburgh 1953), 227.
5. N. Hynd, 'Towards a study of gardening in Scotland from the 16th to the 18th centuries' in D.J. Breeze (ed.), *Studies in Scottish Antiquity* (Edinburgh, 1984), 269–84.
6. J. Blaeu, *Atlas Novus V* (Amsterdam 1654).
7. Sir W. Fraser, *The Sutherland Book* (3 vols., Edinburgh, 1892), 231.
8. Sir W. Fraser, ibid., 363.
9. Sir A. Mitchell (ed.), Geographical collections relating to Scotland made by Walter McFarlane I (Scottish History Society, Edinburgh, 1906), 51, 105.
10. E.H.M. Cox, *A history of gardening in Scotland* (London, 1935).
11. W. Cramond (ed.), *The annals of Banff I* (New Spalding Club, Aberdeen, 1891), 8, 94.
12. W. Cramond, ibid., 41.
13. I.H. Adams, 'The agents of agricultural change' in M.L. Parry and T.R. Slater (eds.), *The making of the Scottish countryside* (London, 1980), 155–75.
14. R.K. Marshall, *The days of Duchess Anne* (London, 1973).
15. T.R. Slater, op.cit., 225.
16. Sir A. Mitchell, op.cit., 26.
17. D. MacGibbon and T. Ross, *The castellated and domestic architecture of Scotland* (Edinburgh, 1887–92).

18. A.H. Millar (ed.), *Glamis book of record* (Scottish History Society, Edinburgh, 1890), 9, 44.
19. J. Macky, *A journey through Scotland* (2nd edition, London, 1729), 135.
20. J. Reid, *The Scots gard'ner* (Edinburgh, 1683), 3.
21. A.A. Tait, *The landscape garden in Scotland 1735-1835* (Edinburgh, 1980), 33-4.
22. Sir A. Mitchell, op.cit., 53.
23. Sir A. Mitchell, op.cit., 53-4.
24. J. Macky, op.cit., 119.
25. Sir A. Mitchell, op.cit., 252.
26. D.W. Kemp, *Tours in Scotland by Richard Pococke* (Scottish History Society, Edinburgh, 1887), 1, 230.
27. C. Cruft, 'James, 2nd Duke of Atholl and John Cheere' in D.J. Breeze (ed.), *Studies in Scottish Antiquity* (Edinburgh, 1984), 285-301.
28. H. Hamilton, *Selections from the Monymusk Papers* (Scottish History Society, Edinburgh, 3rd series, 1945), 39.
29. D.W. Kemp, op.cit., 200.
30. A.A. Tait, op.cit., 58-63.
31. A.A. Tait, idem., 49.
32. C. Cruft, op.cit.
33. T.R. Slater, vide supra.
34. Sir A. Mitchell, op.cit., 241.
35. J. Macky, op.cit., 121.
36. A.A. Tait, op.cit., 73.
37. A.A. Tait, idem., 137.
38. A.A. Tait, idem., 70.
39. A.A. Tait, idem., 39.
40. I.H. Adams, *Peter May, land surveyor, 1752-95* (Scottish History Society, Edinburgh, 4th series, 1979), 15.
41. D.W. Kemp, op.cit., 194.
42. A. and H. Tayler (eds.), *Lord Fife and his factor* (London, 1925), 17.
43. Scottish Record Office, GD 44/52/39, 40.
44. T.R. Slater, op.cit., 240.
45. L. Shaw, *History of the province of Moray enlarged by J.F.S. Gordon* (3 vols. Glasgow, 1882).
46. A.A. Tait, op.cit., 156.
47. I.H. Adams, *The making of urban Scotland* (London, 1978), 68.
48. Sir T. Dick-Lauder (ed.), *Sir Uvedale Price 'On the picturesque'* (London, 1842).
49. D. Lockhart. 'The planned villages' in M.L. Parry and T.R. Slater (eds.), op.cit., 249-70.
50. T.R. Slater, op.cit., 241.
51. Scottish Record Office, GD 44/51/25.

52. Lord Cockburn, *Circuit journeys* (Edinburgh, 1888), 154.
53. H. Woolmer, 'Grantown-on-Spey: an eighteenth century new town', *Town planning review*, 41, 1970, 237–50.
54. I.H. Adams (1978), op.cit., 68.
55. J.C. Loudon, *Encyclopedia of gardening* (5th edition, London, 1828).
56. G. Robertson, *General view of the agriculture of the county of Kincardine* (London, 1813), 58.

THE CONSTRUCTION AND RESTORATION OF THE NORTH EAST TOWER HOUSE

Alistair G. Urquhart, Stonemason, Coull, Aboyne

In the beginning of the 20th century stonemasons in the North East of Scotland were still using boulders as a means of constructing certain buildings. They were working exactly as the masons in previous centuries had done when building the tower houses. There was, of course, a ready supply of boulders which had been liberally distributed around the landscape by the glaciers during the last ice age, and in castles one finds many of the built stones still have dried up lichens and mosses stuck to them. Indeed, had it not been for the glaciers, there is no doubt that the North East's architectural heritage would have looked considerably different.

If boulders had a flat face the masons built them as they came, otherwise a large hammer was used to work them into the required shape. Chippings, known as pinnings, were used as packing so there was no waste. It was a very economical way of building. It appears that large items like lintels and steps were made from basically flat individual stones and dressed to the finished shape. The boulder was, in fact, little more than the concrete block of its day, almost always plastered on the inside of the building and harled on the outside because, as far as castles were concerned, harling was very much the accepted finish.

Foundations

Stone and lime is an immensely strong form of construction weighing in at somewhere around 1¾ tons per cubic yard. The usual wall thickness is 3 feet, sometimes more, and with the average tower house being 50 to 80 feet high one can well imagine the tremendous weights involved. Despite this, foundations were very simply constructed with only the topsoil being removed before building commenced. Often the topsoil is no more than 2–3 inches thick which means that the castle is virtually sitting on the surface. If we were to build a similar tower house today, using traditional stone, we would be required by law to dig deep foundations and pour in many tons of concrete. However, the old castles were far simpler. Glenbuchat, for example, has a course of splayed stones for foundations, but this is by no means standard. Some castles spring from the ground without any foundations at all, while others are set on large boulders projecting beyond the walls to spread the load. Remarkably though, structural cracks from settlement are very rare indeed.

Cracks

One could write a whole book on cracks in castles, but, in my own experience there are only four main types, the most common being the type that starts at the top of the building, goes down the wall and gradually disappears. This is invariably caused by the roof ties rotting and parting company with the rafters. The great weight of slates presses down, forcing the rafters, and consequently the walls, outwards. The second form of crack, the least common of all, starts at the castle's foundation and tapers off as it goes up the wall. These are caused by settlement of some kind and seldom date from the building's early years. They are usually caused by water or human interference undermining the foundations. Before dealing with the other two types of cracks it may be prudent to mention that most of the tower houses have been altered at some time in their life. Usually the windows have been enlarged, their stone arches removed and timber lintels fitted in their place. The third type of crack emanates from the tops of the windows and doors. These may, in fact, be parallel rather than tapering. Decaying timber lintels, either through dry rot or woodworm will most probably be the cause. The final type of crack is often identical in appearance to the third, and can only be identified after extensive investigation. These cracks are caused by the above mentioned alterations when inadequate shoring has been used, allowing the wall to move.

Before any restoration work begins it is imperative to thoroughly

26. Kintore Town House.

27. Recessed pointing on Kintore Town House—a good example of bad pointing!

investigate all cracks and ascertain that all movement has stopped. Only then can repair work commence. The process of 'stitching', as it is called, is relatively simple. Holes are cut at suitable intervals, large stones are built across the cracks and the voids are then packed solid with lime mortar and pinnings. If the cracks are large, 3 inches or more across, they are built up with stone and lime in the conventional manner.

Where there are large voids within the wall, probably caused by rain water running through it, these can usually be grouted up. Grout is basically very thin lime mortar, and when poured into the holes it will find its way into very tiny cracks. I might add at this point that it is extremely important to ensure that there are no lumps in the grout as they can block up the voids before they are properly filled.

Stone Dressing

The 19th century Aberdeen Town House represents an excellent example of Victorian architecture, reflecting as it does details of the North East tower house. It displays perfectionism in craftsmanship, but you will not find granite dressed to this high standard on the old castles. There are, in fact, very good reasons for the difference in finish.

If one looks at Crathes Castle, for example, it will be noted that the old boulder granite used for the dressings has far larger crystals than the denser quarried granite of the Town House. Dense granites are capable of a very fine finish. On the other hand, this cannot readily be achieved with the open textured boulder granites which are really too crumbly.

When it comes to repair and restoration seldom does one see the old granite being used. Instead, masons prefer the more readily available quarried granite. The stone is often machine dressed which gives it a very modern appearance. This, of course, is all to the great detriment of the restored building. One can, however, see quarried granite sympathetically dressed, as at Tillycairn Castle. Here, the architect, Ian Begg, insisted that the stone be hand dressed to give a texture more in keeping with the original, and there is no doubt that to a large extent he has succeeded.

It is not only stonemasons who overdo the craftsmanship. It extends to every trade, and I believe there is a very simple explanation for it all. It is part of a legacy handed down from the Victorians who were absolutely obsessive about perfection. Consequently, for modern craftsmen engaged in restoration, leaving a job that is anything less than perfect in the Victorian sense is unthinkable. The indoctrination was so complete that it is very difficult to cast one's mind back beyond that period. I know that it took me several years to be able to look at tower houses objectively and to dress stones in the style of the period. When you can look at these ancient structures and imagine that you have never heard of the Georgians or Victorians, it is then that you see these buildings in a totally new light. The quality of stonedressing was not the same on every castle, and it seems it was money that set the standard more than anything else.

The Muckrach Castle marriage stone is a good example of medieval carving on a simple castle, and it is fairly obvious from looking at the stone that sandstone was in short supply at Muckrach. The top left hand corner of the stone has been broken off before carving commenced, but this has not deterred them. They have merely moved the top part of the design further to the right. There are several irregularities, like three supposedly identical crowns, none of which are the same. This is almost certainly the work of a mason who spent most of his time building rather than dressing.

Only on castles like Huntly, where there was an ample supply of money, does one see huge amounts of dressed stonework. There, some masons would have been employed to do nothing other than dress. Consequently the standard of the stone dressing is far higher. There are wonderful gargoyles and grotesques on the Castles of Mar, some of which are great fun, if a little risque. Arrowslits are another great source of enjoyment, simple beauty being the appeal of some, while others rely on sophisticated carving. There is an endless supply of interesting little details, and these idiosyncrasies are a continual delight.

Tools

The hammer and puncheon are the granite mason's trade mark, for without these he would cease to exist. These tools, and many others, are still handmade by the blacksmith, and it is a job that requires great skill and knowledge. In Aberdeen there is only one toolsmith left and, as he has no apprentice to carry on the work, what will happen when this man retires I do not know.

Many of the tools we use have not changed for centuries. However, power saws are now available with diamond tipped blades, which have greatly speeded up the work. These saws can now cut granite without water lubrication, so it is possible to cut stone *in situ* almost anywhere in a building. Also, most chisels now have tungsten tips, which means a much longer time between sharpening. All this makes the cutting of stone far cheaper which represents tremendous savings to would-be restorers, making the whole thing much more attractive.

Slating

Most of the North East castles have slated roofs and most, it seems, have the old Scots slates. These vary from mid to dark blue and many have delightful ochre coloured veining. Drum Castle is one good example.

There are, of course, exceptions. Leslie Castle (1661) apparently had green slate when it was first built, and we also know that part of Aboyne Castle was at one time roofed with green slate. When Leslie was restored it was re-roofed with new green Cumberland slate, this colour of slate being unavailable elsewhere. There is, however, a penalty to be paid when using new slate, for they are rather lacking in texture. In this respect there is no comparison between the old and the new. The main roof at the back of Castle Fraser, when seen about lunch time with the sun shining on it at right angles, cannot fail to impress. Its texture is such a joy to behold.

The old tower houses had no guttering, the rain water simply ran straight off the roofs on to the ground. To avoid the problem of water constantly running down the walls, the bottom course of slates had a large projection, 5 to 7 inches, which helped to throw the water clear of the walls, and carved stone guttering was used to channel the rainwater away at ground level. On a modern building, with guttering fitted, the slate projection is more like 2 to 3 inches. The general belief is that the North East castle, when first built, had slated roofs with leaded valleys. There are those who say maybe, and the longer I work on these castles the more convinced I become that the maybe's are right!

28. Over-dressed granite of the dense small grained type.

29. A slated valley between two roof angles at Beldorney Castle.

Take Crathes Castle, for example. Leaded valleys everywhere, but there is good evidence to suggest that these valleys may have been slated originally. When lead was recently being renewed near the belfry, stone guttering was found underneath the old lead, a good indication that lead was not used when the castle was first constructed.

Castle Fraser, on the other hand, still has some slated valleys. But what of the big round tower with its flat roof? Surely it must have been leaded to keep out the water? Well, it is thought that originally it had stone slabs laid directly on to a timber beamed roof, thus obviating the need for lead, and certainly we know of many roofs of this type. Craigievar Castle could also have been completely slated and 'lead-free'.

Was lead too expensive? Yes, no doubt for some it was, but if anyone could have afforded lead, the Marquis of Huntly could. Yet even in his magnificent palace built 1597–1602, many devices have been constructed in stone to deal with the problem of water running off roofs. One can see clearly that around chimneys, turrets and towers, channels cut from stone have been made to do the work that lead did in later years. In country areas, at least, it would seem that lead was the exception rather than the rule.

When I was engaged in the restoration work at Beldorney Castle I investigated the condition of the original plasterwork. It was when removing the top coat of Victorian plaster that I discovered grafitti underneath. Scratched on a wall in the Priest's room was what appeared to be a man with a kilt, walking stick and dog, usually referred to by the tradesmen who worked on the castle as 'the little mannie wi' the dog'! There are also initials and a date 1674. The plaster was badly eroded and looked as if water had been running down the walls.

Now, assuming this date of 1674 to be correct, why would the castle have been in such bad condition after little more than 100 years? Well, the present roof, complete with slated valleys, and again no lead, is said to date from early 1700. Perhaps this was the first time it had ever been slated. It may well have been thatched originally and its owners unable to afford to have it redone.

They do say that a good heather thatch will last 100 years, which would fit in with the grafitti date. Further to this point a considerable amount of composted material was found on top of the wallheads, all consistent with the building having been originally thatched.

Davidston House, near Keith, is perhaps one of the best examples of a slated roof without lead anywhere in the North East. This roof is also said to date from the 1700s. Looking up from the courtyard one can see a large and very impressive swept valley. On the other sides of the house there are two turrets and several dormer windows, all slated, with not an ounce of lead to be seen anywhere. Nevertheless, this kind of slating is by no means unique to Scotland. But, when I first saw the roof at Davidston, with its old Scots slates which are rather thick, almost crude, being treated in such a skilled manner, I found it a very humbling experience.

Looking at some records we find that in 1380 a plumber, William of Tweedale, burgess of Anderstone (St Andrews) was asked to do leadwork to the roof at the Abbey of Arbroath, and that in 1506 an English plumber was contracted to do roofing work to the church of the new University in Aberdeen. These are only two examples selected at random, but it would seem reasonable to conclude that plumbers were in short supply.

But I do not believe that this alone was the reason for the lack of lead in the rural North East. St Andrews, Arbroath and Aberdeen were all seaports, whilst inland roads were virtually non-existent, making transport extremely difficult. So perhaps it was the coming of the turnpikes in the early 1800s that made lead readily available for building construction in the rural North East. Before any real conclusion can be drawn, a considerable amount of further research is required.

Coming back to the present day, occasionally one hears of slated valleys still being ripped out and replaced with lead. But more usually they are repaired or renewed. When it comes to restoring ruined castles I have never heard of anyone restoring a slated valley. They are always done in lead. This is principally because it is difficult to find anyone who can execute the work and, more important, lead is believed to be correct.

Pointing

By the end of the 1800s there were thousands of highly skilled craftsmen, yet barely a hundred years later there are hardly any who could be classed as skilled craftsmen in the original sense of the word. Centuries of tradition is being forgotten and nowhere is this more evident than in pointing.

In all fairness it must be said that the Historic Buildings and Monuments Department do a marvellous job, and were it not for them we would have little architectural heritage left. They provide grants, impart a lot of valuable information, and prevent over-zealous restorers from redesigning buildings. In the majority of cases they really are indispensable. But, when it comes to pointing, they completely ignore what has gone before and try to impose new ideas imported from south of the border. Many of the older masons are hostile to these ideas and, I believe, quite rightly so, as not only is the character of these listed buildings being changed, but the skills associated with the original pointing are also being lost.

Although the Ancient Monuments Department claim they have no policy on pointing, almost every building in their care gets the same clone-like treatment which, incidentally, costs considerably more to execute than the traditional pointing. A further worrying aspect is that the National Trust for Scotland has also embraced this recessed pointing which, with all its variants, is very much a 20th century creation and, in my opinion, cannot truthfully be classed as conservation.

Flushing off the wall has always been the stonemason's objective. It kept out the weather and was cheap and simple to do. Stonemasons have practised this successful form of pointing the world over for countless centuries. Why, then, has it suddenly been decided that it is not suitable? Quite frankly, I am baffled. Undoubtedly the most depressing aspect of all this is the fact that flush pointing could completely disappear and no one will know that such a thing existed.

Rightly or wrongly, there is no denying that many see recessed pointing as aesthetically superior to the old flush pointing. There is no doubt that it is very tidy and inoffensive, but should we be putting cosmetics before conservation? After all, aesthetics have nothing to do with conservation. Even though one may believe some piece of work to be hideous, one cannot pretty it up. It must be preserved as it is.

30. Stone guttering which gathered water shed from the large north tower at Huntly Castle. The runoff drops from here onto the wallhead, and thence spouts to the ground.

31. The image of the 'little man and the dog' on plaster at Beldorney Castle.

Harling

Harling, although not exclusive to Scotland, is a very important part of Scotland's architectural history. It is mentioned in records as far back as the 15th century but could certainly be considerably older. It was continued on through the centuries and was extensively practised right up until the 1960s when, like stonemasonry, it virtually stopped.

Many people think that there is too much harling going on at the present day but, in fact, what they are seeing is not harling but dry dashing. This is an English import and a modern one at that, and is nothing more than crushed stone thrown on to wet cement plaster.

The traditional Scottish harling, however, consists generally of rough sand, lime, and nowadays cement is usually added. This is mixed up into a wet slurry and hurled at the wall. It all looks very easy, but to achieve a good result requires a considerable degree of skill. If truth be told, there really is very little harling going on at present, and were it not for the Historic Buildings Council and their insistence that buildings be re-harled, there is grave doubt as to whether the craft would survive.

The vast majority of tradesmen hate harling because it is a horrible filthy job. The splashes of harling dry up your skin and burn your eyes. It is hard, sweaty work and there is really nothing good that can be said for it. But, for all that, once the work has been completed it is a great feeling just to stand back and admire your efforts. Of course, there are always a few blemishes to annoy you, but one must simply put this down to the fact that the whole thing has been done by hand.

One of harling's great attributes is its sculptural quality. When a building has been harled you are no longer looking at individual stones, but something more akin to a giant sculpture, and this is particularly true in the case of tower houses.

Castle Fraser, it could be said, is something of an oddity, being half harled and half pointed. This castle was, of course, like all the other North East castles, originally completely harled. I am told that it was Douglas Simpson, the historian, who instigated the removal of the harling some time before the National Trust took the castle on. If, for no other reason, it is interesting to see the bare stone, the skeleton as it were. However, I cannot say that I care for

32. A painted plaster wall with stylised horse and borders revealed in the Priest's Room, Beldorney Castle.

33. Board-marked plaster at Beldorney Castle. The radiating ridges mark the positions of the board edges.

this sort of thing. I much prefer to see adherence to the creator's original concept, being firmly of the belief that you cannot improve on great work.

Drum Castle used to be a rather ghastly indescribable pink, but when the National Trust for Scotland came along they soon changed all that. It has now been re-harled a shade of light yellow ochre, a very subtle and natural-looking colour, best seen in the morning light. Drum is the place to see harling at work. You can see harled crowsteps, harled window ingoes, you can see harling used to highlight dressed stonework, and a gable at the east side where everything is harled. It is pure Scottish magic. A complete success story for the National Trust for Scotland.

Plastering

Beldorney Castle was, in many ways, one of the most interesting buildings I have ever worked on. When I first visited the castle, immediately prior to its restoration, it was a rather sombre, unassuming grey structure. But over the years, as work progressed, we made some interesting discoveries which offered up a considerable amount of information.

One such discovery was the board-marked plaster on the ceilings of the barrel vaults. There has always been some debate as to whether these tower houses were pointed or plastered. The general consensus in recent times usually favoured the latter, that is conventional trowel applied plaster. Huntly Castle appears to be one good example of this. The board-marked plaster, as we shall see, is considerably different, and I believe a much more likely finish on many buildings.

Nevertheless, to grasp the thinking behind this idea one must first understand how a vault is made. Before a vault can be constructed a wooden mould, consisting of boarding supported by a framework, has to be built to the shape of the intended vault. Once this has been achieved building then commences at the bottom of the mould and continues until the entire mould has been covered.

Now, whether the mould was first coated with building lime, or whether the lime simply ran through the stones on to the boards, is not entirely clear. The fact remains that once you remove the mould you are left with 'board-marked plaster'. The question then arises as to whether this so called board-marked plaster was considered a good enough finish, or was it in fact plastered over?

At Beldorney the board-marked ceiling had been painted from the time of construction, so it would appear to have been quite acceptable. On the upper floors at Beldorney the walls were completely painted from top to bottom with a rich variety of designs and colours. The ground floor, on the other hand, only had a passageway painted and this had solid brown walls and a solid black board marked ceiling which was unbelievably dark and dingy. But as the ground floor area had been mostly used for servants, this would no doubt have been considered quite adequate for them. Indeed, plasterwork on most ground floor areas is often less well finished, with trowel marks clearly visible. Pitcaple Castle also has some excellent examples of vaults with well preserved board-marked plaster, but in this instance unpainted.

The finishing of the plaster is another highly contentious area. Was it rough or was it smooth? I have heard some heated arguments over this. The great problem here, of course, is where do you find a building with original plasterwork? Most of it has been covered up with later plaster or, much more likely, it has fallen off the walls.

Returning to Beldorney again, here we were most fortunate. Because the timber panelling had been added later the old plaster was still underneath and in reasonably good condition. A detailed examination revealed that it had been applied rather sparingly so that the tops of the stones were covered, but only just. The walls are never dead flat like 20th century plasterwork. Instead the plaster has the effect of being allowed to flow over the stonework. To remove trowel marks a fine haired brush has been used and the brush marks are clearly visible. This technique is still used today in some instances. Huntly Castle, along with a few others that still have preserved samples, give a good indication that this must surely have been the standard method of the times.

Garderobes

When one speaks of toilets one is frequently accused of indulging in lavatorial humour. Be that as it may, toilets are a very necessary part of human life and I must confess that I find the earlier attempts fascinating.

34. To harl or not to harl? That is the question at Castle Fraser.

At Beldorney Castle we uncovered three, all of which had been
built up in the earlier 1700s. The Beldorney garderobes, as they
are more commonly known, are of the variety which have a shaft
within the wall. Both emerge a few feet from the back door. I say
both, as the garderobe in the Priest's room and the one in the room
below share the same shaft. The lack of privacy when using these
garderobes, and the strong upward draught, must have quickly
diminished any thoughts of lingering. The garderobe in the
Priest's room, being larger, does at least provide some degree of
seclusion, and perhaps the draught was stopped by straw at the
bottom of the shaft. It is what one might call a more user-friendly
version.

At the present day the whole idea of these garderobes and their
close proximity to the back door is hard to contemplate. The fact
that the shafts were permanently coated with excreta must have
left visitors to the castle in no doubt as to their existence, whether
they saw them or not. This may well have been reason enough for
the Georgians to build them up.

It is interesting to remember that dry toilets without any
chemicals were used until comparatively recently in many
agricultural communities. The toilet situated reasonably close to
the dwelling house was used till the bucket filled up. Its contents
was then consigned to the adjoining midden and this, in turn, was
emptied annually and spread on the land as manure to grow food.
This continued on one farm that I knew right up until the end of
the 1950s. Seen in this context, garderobes become altogether less
repugnant.

Timberwork

In the earlier tower houses like Terpersie and Beldorney (mid
1500s) there was not a great deal of timber to speak of. Floors,
roofs, windows and doors just about sums it up. Craigievar, on the
other hand (1626) was considerably different with some panelling
and built-in furniture being provided at the outset.

Earlier castles like Beldorney had panelling added in later
centuries to bring them into fashion. How much of this went on we
will never know as so much has been destroyed in later modernisa-
tion programmes. During restoration work on some castles one
discovers various pieces of very old timber mouldings which

35 (a) The economical use of freestone for square and round angle turret corbelling as well as corner masonry at Glenbuchat Castle. Angled shot loops provided covering fire by small arms towards the wall base.

(b) The *trompe* (supporting arch) for the salient turret at Glenbuchat Castle. Note how the external base of the castle sits on a line of large boulders, lying virtually on the soil surface, and protruding proud of the external wall face.

resemble nothing on the existing castle. These finds, though very interesting, are extremely frustrating, as we seldom discover their original purpose.

Scots pine is by far the most common timber in the castles. The much talked about oak is seldom seen, Tilquhillie Castle, near Banchory, being a rare exception. Here all the roof timbers are oak, and being used to seeing nothing but pine, I found the experience very stimulating.

The most interesting use for timber that I have ever seen was undoubtedly at Muckrach Castle where it was used to reinforce the stone and lime walls. This was, without doubt in my mind, the product of a society that believed in a timber technology. There has never been an abundance of stone masons on Speyside. Timber workers have reigned supreme! When the masons arrived to build Muckrach Castle, they had evidently to take second place. Timber had been built into the walls of the turrets and also under the corbelling. The two storey cap house had massive beams built into the walls immediately above the corbelling, and when I arrived to restore Muckrach little remained of these rotten beams. The cap house was sitting on almost nothing and was extremely dangerous. It needed quite a few cups of coffee before I made any move to repair it. In modern jargon this is known as a 'life threatening situation', and anyway I was simply taking the advice of an old stonemason whose motto was 'when in doubt brew up'!

This belief in timber is also clearly seen in some of the old cottages on Speyside, where a framework of timber beams was first erected, then the stonework was built around the beams, each time timber being considered more important than stone. This, of course, was completely contradictory to the normal way of thinking and it is an idea that the old stone masons must have found very hard to accept.

Ironwork

In the building of the tower house, the blacksmith's craft was just as important as any other, but today the work of these artisans has almost been forgotten. When one visits an old building very seldom is the ironwork pointed out, no matter how good it is. The only thing you are likely to hear about is the iron yett.

Blacksmithing today has completely changed. Modern electric

36. The tools of the stone-mason, including (bottom left to right): *catchie* hammer which is multi-purpose but used specifically for tapping in pinnings; *mell* hammer for dressing granites and a blocking hammer used for preliminary shaping down, in some cases, the final shaping of big stones. Also displayed are a selection of puncheons (chisels), used for ripping out mortar prior to removal of single stones, and for dressing stone.

welding means that few blacksmiths will ever learn firework, which was so necessary for the creation of the castles' iron fittings. Just how many present day smiths could make a yett? Very few, I would guess.

There is little good smithing work being done in the castles today, and much of what one sees has a distinctly agricultural feel to it. By the time most restoration jobs are ready for ironwork money is usually in short supply and there is not enough left to pay for decent fittings. Even when there is the required finance, finding a good blacksmith with the necessary skill and knowledge is well nigh impossible. I have only once seen new ironwork in the Scottish style that stood up to scrutiny, and that was made by a blacksmith from the north of England.

Sadly, during restoration, a great deal of original ironwork is often destroyed. Many fittings are fixed to rotten timber and usually look a bit rusty, consequently they frequently land on the bonfire. Of all the old trades that have suffered in recent times, blacksmithing has undoubtedly suffered the most, and attitudes will have to alter dramatically before there are any positive changes in this area of restoration.

Conclusion

The solid fortified design of the tower house was without doubt a product of troubled times, but money, status, transport availability of materials and the necessary skills were the factors that determined the final creation. They all used the same ingredients but variations in the recipe ensured that no two castles were the same.

TOWER HOUSE RESTORATION
IN SCOTLAND

Marc Ellington[1]

Driving through remote Scottish countryside searching for a ruined tower house suitable for restoration is an experience common to many of the newer proprietors of some of Scotland's finest early domestic buildings. With an Ordnance Survey map perched on the dashboard and all five volumes of MacGibbon & Ross's *Castellated and Domestic Architecture of Scotland* (1887–92) sliding across the rear seat, would-be restorers set out in search of that long abandoned, ivy-covered ruin which, with a high degree of vision, determination and hard work, could become their home.

Valuable assistance from Kitty Cruft at the National Monument Record Office in Edinburgh, and the continuing encouragement of great men such as David Walker and Stewart Cruden, have led a new generation of restorers down the 'deep rutted farm track', described by Nigel Tranter in his *Fortified House in Scotland* (also five volumes), towards a 'sadly neglected tower, not beyond resurrection'.

Locating the building is only the first step. Ruins worthy of restoration are frequently within farming units, part of a large estate or sometimes near later, occupied buildings, often making purchase difficult. The situation can be further complicated if the structure is the seat from which the owner of the estate derives his or her baronial designation but this can be overcome by the present feudal baron retaining ownership of the caput baronae in the form of a few square feet of ground on which the tower sits. Fortunately, the court of the Lord Lyon in Edinburgh, which issues judgements concerning such matters, has constantly taken a positive view of restoration work. From the 14th century through to the middle 1600s the tower house was the chosen dwelling of those with something to protect or the need to convince all that

77

they did. Merchants and clerics as well as landowners, built and lived in fortified houses. In early buildings, defensive considerations were foremost, resulting in tall, strong towers, vaulted at ground-floor level, massive walls peppered with shotholes and gunloops and crowned with a corbelled parapet providing an angle of fire to protect the single entrance door. By the end of the fifteenth century the influence of Continental fashion, the desire for greater domestic comfort and the diminishing need for defence encouraged the development of more complex layouts. Although retaining strength, the later structures possess far greater elaboration in design and detailing than the earlier basic tower, with defensive features often becoming more decorative than functional.

Long after the great Elizabethan country houses were an accepted part of the English countryside, Scottish masons were still at work carving shotholes and gunloops in the walls of what were to be some of Scotland's finest tower houses. While some parts of the country remained lawless and dangerous well into the 18th century, it was the symbolic value of the tower house as the residence of a man of substance rather than its inherent strength as a fortification that more convincingly explains its remaining in favour.

Simple tower, L plan, Z plan and the later T plan are the four basic design types, but distinct regional variations exist—from the Border keep and the early curtain-walled castles of the west to the later, complex towers of Aberdeenshire and Kincardineshire. Local schools of master masons working within a limited geographical area for clients frequently united through family, political or religious ties also provide rich regional variations in the buildings they erected, extended or elaborated. Nowhere is this more clearly seen than in the North-East, where two generations of the Bel family of master masons left their signature in the exuberant upper works of buildings such as Craigievar, Crathes, Midmar and Castle Fraser.

From the 1820s a growing enthusiasm for Scottish baronial architecture manifested itself as part of the general nationalistic and romantic revival of interest in national architecture and identity which swept through Europe. It replaced the English Tudor and Gothic styles which had hitherto characterised castle-style country houses in Scotland. What the writings of Sir

Walter Scott established, the building of Balmoral confirmed. Scottish baronial style became the architectural hallmark of the age. The spirit and values of nineteenth century Britain also harmonised well with the symbolic values embodied in the Scottish baronial or tower house style.

Despite this Victorian enthusiasm, an alarming number of important buildings were either demolished or allowed to fall into hopeless ruin during the nineteenth century. While early examples of active preservation are few, a nucleus of interest and concern did exist. As early as 1824 John Smith, the Aberdeen architect who was to transform Balmoral for Sir Robert Gordon and whose son William rebuilt it for the Prince Consort, wrote to Sir John Forbes regarding his tower of Craigievar: 'the castle is well worth being preserved as it is one of the finest specimens in the country of the age and style in which it was built'.

In a considerable number of vigorous nineteenth century country house expansions, tower houses were retained as an element, though often becoming almost completely engulfed in the later 'improvements'. This cocooning of early towers within later building works was often the means of their survival. The publication by R.W. Billings and the monumental survey work of MacGibbon & Ross combined to increase general public interest in the tower house as an important architectural type and heralded what was to be a growing concern for its future care and preservation.

By the end of the nineteenth century an increasing number of tower houses were being constructed with little or no compromise to their original form. Indeed even roofless ruins such as Cairnbulg, in Aberdeenshire, and Old Place of Mochrum, in Ayrshire were undergoing complete refurbishment for occupation—Cairnbulg in 1896 for Sir John Duthie, a shipbuilder from the North East, Old Place of Mochrum in 1873 for the Marquis of Bute. Through his pioneering work at Earlshall (Fife), Balmanno (Perthshire) and Dundarave (Argyll), Sir Robert Lorimer carried into this century what has become a tradition of respect for and an understanding of, the architectural importance of the tower house.

The attractive sculptural qualities of these buildings, their relatively modest size and the current enthusiasm for historic architecture, combined with the increasing difficulties of staffing, maintenance and heating larger 18th and 19th century country houses, has helped to bring about a reassessment of the positive and practical values of the tower house as an easily managed family home. Now the tower house is once more fashionable contradicting the comment made by the Earl of Strathmore in 1677, that 'such houses are truly quite out of fashion as feuds are'.

Since the mid 1950s, in excess of 50 ruined or substantially derelict tower houses have undergone major reconstruction, bringing new life and a future to buildings that might otherwise have been lost. The Historic Buildings Council for Scotland has actively supported most recent major tower reconstructions. When one compares the relatively modest outlay of providing grants against the cost, for example, of taking buildings into state guardianship, there can be little doubt that the taxpayer has received good value.

This recent burst of activity is remarkable, not only for the number of buildings saved and the standards of workmanship employed, but also for the marked difference in approach adopted by most of the new restorers. Most of the reconstructions undertaken in the later years of the nineteenth century up until the Second World War were evolved and supervised by architects working for client occupiers with a varying degree of direct personal involvement in their project. In contrast many recent restorations have been almost entirely controlled and directed by the owners themselves using their architects and professional advisers principally for the purpose of providing working drawings and communicating with relevant public authorities. This degree of personal involvement and commitment by owners has contributed greatly to their restorations' success and individuality.

As most recently restored tower houses lack formal and highly finished later interiors, the scope for creative internal treatment is enormous. While many restorers have opted for white painted plaster walls and period oak furniture, some buildings—including Kinkell, in Easter Ross, and Cleish, in Kinross—have successfully absorbed high-quality contemporary fittings, pictures and sculpture. The cellular simplicity of the vaulted ground floor and the gaunt, stark proportions of the interiors of the upper levels of most fortified houses lack the period connotations of many 18th and 19th century buildings, giving them a remarkably timeless quality rarely found in British houses.

The difficulty of locating competent stonemasons, plasterers, slaters, and other tradesmen with traditional skills, particularly in rural areas, has become an increasing problem. Yet this recent upsurge in reconstruction has also swelled the numbers of skilled craftsmen. A tower house restoration presents an ideal opportunity for tradesmen to develop, improve and exercise traditional skills.

For a stonemason to have the opportunity of revaulting a great hall ceiling or a slater the challenge of dressing and laying fish-tail slates on a turret roof, is an experience not to be found in a lifetime of normal repair work. The experience gained and the skills learned by craftsmen and their apprentices working on these restorations will benefit Scotland's historic and traditional buildings for years to come. Who would have imagined that some Victorian baronial pile might owe its future survival to skills learned by a tradesman while working on the restoration of a 16th century tower house, which provided its 19th century architect with his original inspiration?

While excellent results have been achieved, it could be considered risky for so much reconstruction work to have proceeded when so little was known of how tower houses were originally constructed, decorated, furnished or lived in. Serious academic work is lacking to assist our understanding of many aspects of this important national building type. *The Scottish Castle* by Stewart Cruden stands virtually alone as an authoritative work on the subject.

An example of an important area where further research would benefit restoration concerns the finishing of external walls with harling, the surface rendering lime mortar orginally applied to most towers. Almost nothing is known of how harling was initially carried out, its composition or the way it would have looked on a newly constructed building.

In the absence of authoritative guidance, a practice has been universally accepted and adopted of rendering buildings with an even, sugar-icing type of lime harl, the smoother the better. While not always unattractive in a hobbity sort of way, this has no historical basis. Hopefully, as more research is directed towards the many questions surrounding harling, we will witness improved standards in this most important and highly visible aspect of tower-house restoration work.

Given the lack of information available concerning many aspects of reconstruction work, it is perhaps not surprising that a

number of tower-house restorers have themselves become considerable authorities in various areas. This has led to the establish-
ment of a network for the exchange of information between
restorers, craftsmen, and architects directly involved.

Questions as varied as 'Where can I get best Caithness paving
slabs?', 'Who can advise on the best way to revault a passage?', or
'Who's good at doing complex roof leadwork?' arise when two or
more restorers gather. Free exchange of information has been vital
in explaining the growing body of knowledge which has steadily
built up over recent years. As a direct result, we are now
witnessing a pattern of increasing quality with the completion of
each new project.

The Historic Buildings Council for Scotland has provided help
in this field, not only through its vital grant support, but also in the
advice and guidance freely given by its highly knowledgeable and
helpful staff. A usual condition of grant support is the agreement
by the restorer to allow a degree of public access to the buildings,
but most owners are justifiably proud of their restorations and
take delight in showing those interested what has been achieved.

To all with a concern for the care and preservation of Scotland's
architectural heritage, there can be little that is more heartening
than to witness the new life given to a recently restored tower
house, which just a few years before appeared beyond hope. It is
easy to imagine the satisfaction shared by a present day restorer
and the 16th century tower house builder who wrote:

> This undertaken and begoun at Whitsonday in an 1590 but would
> never have been perfyted giff the bountiful hand of my God had
> nocht maid me to take the work in hand myselff, and furnished
> strangelie to my consideration all things neidfull, so that never week
> passed but all sort of workmen was well peyit, never a dayes
> intermission fra the beginning to the compleiting of it, and never a
> soar finger during the haill labour. In Junie begoun and in the
> monethe of March eftir I was resident therein . . . thair for justile I
> may call it a speckyakle of god's liberalite.

[1]   The author is a member of the Historic Buildings Council for
Scotland, a trustee of the Scottish Historic Buildings Trust and
Scotland's representative on the British Heritage Commission.

AN APPRAISAL OF THE RESTORATION OF CERTAIN NORTH EAST CASTLES

Colin Coutts[1]

Before discussing specific examples of restoration, it is necessary to outline the reasons behind the existence of so many castles in Scotland and to summarise their evolution and development. Subsequently an appraisal of particular restorations will be made, including the reasons stimulating them and their degree of success.

Historical Background

The abortive Edwardian campaigns left an indelible mark upon the architecture of Scotland and the north of England. From the fourteenth century onwards, for more than two hundred years, every lord's or squire's hall north of the Tees had reason to be a strong fortalice. It was because of this social climate that the initially Norman tradition of a square keep or tower house was employed in North Britain. Previous to this period the norm had been a hall built of timber, wattle and daub or stone, with private rooms at one end and kitchens and offices at the other. In some cases, due to unrest or disturbances, this hall was simply enclosed with a fortified curtain wall. Where the house was to be built from scratch, it was sensible to design it as a strong fortalice. These tower houses were neither great fortresses nor strongholds of mighty feudal lords, but the dwellings of intermediate and minor landowners. For landowners of modest resources, the simple rectangular tower was the most convenient and defensible residence.

In Scotland, the tower house remained the characteristic form for a laird's 'house of fence' until far into the seventeenth century.

No other nation has developed the tower house theme to a greater extent or evolved such a variety of designs.

Characteristics and construction of the tower house

Among the Scottish tower houses an increasing conflict became apparent between the primary need for defence and a subsequent and necessary wish for comfort. Defensive strength could not be maintained unless comfort was entirely precluded. This was because complete defence called for walls of enormous thickness (2.1m–3.4m) with few and narrow windows, doors at first floor level reached by a removable ladder and gloomy, stone-vaulted, fireproof interiors. Should comfort be sought through the provision of large, conveniently disposed windows and ground level entrance door, defensive strength was considerably reduced. A state of tension, therefore, existed in later tower houses between the two requirements of strength and convenience.

Another stress was created by the need to provide for firearm defence. Small arms, which could be used within the confines of a narrow building, came into general use about the middle of the sixteenth century. The tower house had progressively grown in height, both to provide greater safety for the defenders from missiles, and to reduce the ground area of the wall face potentially exposed to the sapper's tools. With the general introduction of firearms the axis of defence changed from the vertical to the horizontal. This meant the defence of the tower house took place through gunloops provided in flanking towers or wings rather than from the wall-head.

In these later fortified houses, comfort and defence now acted together. The flanking features added to defend the main structure with musketry also provided extra accommodation. Due to their diagonally-opposed positioning, the flanking towers interfered as little as possible with the admission of daylight and were eventually elaborated into a characteristic upper-level development with corbelling and conically roofed turrets.

The 'batter' of the walls of Scottish tower houses is a typical feature. The outer face of the wall is never actually vertical and the wall-planes are ingathered as they rise, this being accentuated in the upper two-thirds of the structure. Great thickness of masonry is not needed for defence at the higher levels. Relief is also given to the oversailing parapet without giving the building a top-heavy appearance. The defenders above, due to the inward slope of the wall, do not require to expose themselves when repelling attackers at the base. This 'entasis' is one of the tower house's most subtly attractive features.

The entrance of a tower house was always strongly defended. The norm was an outer wooden door with an inner iron gate, both held closed by stout wooden draw-bars. The timber door was made up in two pieces, the front of vertical and the back of horizontal boards, all clinched together using iron nails. The inner iron gate, or 'yett' to give it the Scottish terminology, was placed so close behind the timber door as to prevent the latter being opened without the release of the former. The yett itself was constructed using interlacing iron bars, the ingenious connection of which lent great strength to the gate. This structural technique was never copied south of the Border in England. The practice there was to pass all the vertical bars in front of the horizontals. The whole framework was then riveted or clasped together and boarded up on both sides, in front with vertical and behind with horizontal boards.

In early times all the windows were protected by 'grilles' or iron gratings constructed in the same interlocking fashion as the yetts. This often projected in the form of a cage, for the better protection of the window. From the fifteenth century onwards, it became common practice to provide the upper two-thirds of window apertures with leaded glass and the lower third with inward-opening wooden shutters. This allowed both daylighting and ventilation to take place simultaneously.

Development of the tower house

There is a great variety of type amongst the later Scottish tower houses. Both the simple rectangular and the L-plan continued in use until the seventeenth century. Some of these differ little from their precursors of the fourteenth century, but others, whilst adhering to the basic ancestral design, are more advanced in comfort. One advantage of the L-plan tower, is the strong position for the entrance door in the re-entrant angle protected by the limbs of the building. This strategic siting of the door allowed its placing at ground rather than first floor level. Although the whole wing in

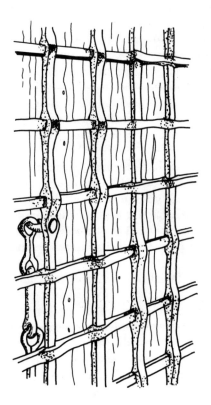

37. Yett.

the L-plan may have housed the stair from ground to first floor level, access from there usually continued in a smaller turnpike stair contained in a turret. A later sophistication was to extrude the stair tower in the re-entrant angle. All were to allow the wing to house rooms appropriately subordinate to those in the main block.

With the introduction of flanking defence by ground floor gunloops, the castle responded by a process of lateral expansion, towers being placed to sweep the faces of the main house or to cover the rear where the courtyard wall could not provide a defence. The logical conclusion resulted in the characteristic Scottish Z-plan castle. This consisted of a rectangular main block with a tower placed at two diagonally-opposed corners. Each tower flanked two sides of the main block and that block provided cover for the towers. This arrangement made it impossible to approach the castle from any direction without coming under fire. Different combinations can be found. The flanking towers are sometimes round, sometimes square, and in other instances one round and one square. There are also towers which start round at ground level and are corbelled out above into rectangular cap-houses.

The ideal aims of restoration

As castles have endured hundreds of years of turmoil and unrest, they have come to symbolise certain worthwhile and sought after qualities. As already indicated, the tower house has evolved principally as a place of strength and security. Although this physical defensive strength is redundant in these relatively law abiding times, a mental security or refuge from the rigours and pressures of modern life may be desirable. Through strength, a feeling of power is given, and from that, prestige; this has always been an undeniable aspect of living in a castle.

A strong link with tradition is also an appealing reason for a tower house to be restored for habitation. This is obviously because its longevity supplies a tangible link with the past and with history, again implying feelings of comfort and belonging. The romance of the idea of having a castle to live in is also an encouraging motive towards restoration.

In addition, a straightforward love of old buildings is required, along with a desire to preserve a piece of history and prevent it deteriorating into oblivion. Romantic though the notion may be, living in a restored tower house is definitely not the kind of existence which would suit everyone. There are problems related to the very qualities and advantages which a tower house evokes.

Ideally a tower house or castle restoration would recreate the original building down to the last detail with as much authenticity as historical knowledge allows. This is where potential conflict arises. Obviously, the evolution of the tower house design has meant that in order to provide strength, security and defensibility, sacrifices have been made in domestic convenience. The purposes of the original tower house design differ markedly from today's home requirements. A relative lack of sophistication by modern standards means that substantial compromises must be made during the restoration if an adequate standard of domestic comfort is to be achieved. This is a fine balance because incorporating modern amenities within the tower house could result in a complete destruction of its character.

Towie-Barclay Castle—its history and restoration

Towie-Barclay was completely ruinous when Mr and Mrs Marc Ellington bought it in 1970, with the aim of restoring it. Towie-Barclay was the first of a spate of castle restorations carried out in the North East in the past two decades. In 1972, after twenty months hard work the former empty shell was restored to its present condition.

The castle is an L-plan tower house situated near Auchterless, belonging to a group of three similar castles, namely Gight, Craig and Delgaty. The close proximity of their dates of construction in 'the third quarter of the sixteenth century'[2] and their similarity of plan and detail allows the assumption that the same master mason was responsible for them all. The individual dates of construction suggest that Towie Barclay was the latest to be completed, as a date stone in the wall gives the date 1593. Each of the castles in the group possesses stone groined and ribbed vaulting.

Entry to the castle is gained through the main arched doorway, placed just off the re-entrant angle, opening into a small Gothic ribbed and vaulted entrance vestibule. The arms and initials of Sir Patrick Barclay, the laird responsible for the erection of the castle, are carved on the central boss of the entrance vestibule's vault.

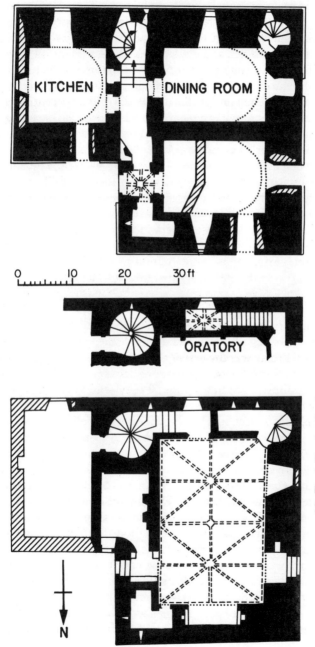

KITCHEN

DINING ROOM

ORATORY

0   10   20   30 ft

N

38. Towie Barclay Castle: upper – plan of ground floor: lower – plan of first floor.

The doorway is defended by a gunloop in the re-entrant angle, the internal splay of which is protected by a masonry column. The whole ground floor is protected on all sides by gun-loops. From the entrance vestibule, a tunnel-vaulted passage leads off to the left, terminating in four steps before the main turnpike stair commences. From this vaulted passage the original barrel-vaulted kitchen is reached on the left, and to the right are the dining room and bedrooms in the former cellars which are also barrel-vaulted. From the dining room a private stair ascends to the hall.

At first floor level, is the great late-Gothic hall, measuring nine metres long, six metres wide and six metres high. The hall is the most important and noted feature of the castle. The ceiling is divided into two bays, each of which is vaulted. The ribs spring from decoratively carved corbels set mid-way up the walls and there are three bosses at their intersections. From the hall, a private stair leads up to an oratory, set in the thickness of the south gable of the hall. This oratory has its own ribbed and groined vault and is open to the hall, separated from it by a screen of five pierced quatrefoils. The oratory is, therefore, in the same form and position as a traditional minstrels' gallery, in relation to the hall. From the hall two further rooms can be reached, and the fireplace is in the north gable, as is usual. Above the kitchen, in the jamb of the L-plan, more bedrooms are to be found, reached from the main stair.

To complete the description of the castle as it stands today, it must be noted that a two-storey caphouse was added on top of the castle. This was not part of the original restoration but was carried out a few years later. The addition of this caphouse is an example of the conflict between comfort and authenticity. A caphouse had been there at one time, and, as indicated by foundation stones and heightened chimney gables, a further two storeys, removed in the eighteenth century. Whilst it would have been a less controversial option not to build afresh upon the existing and now restored lower two storeys, the accommodation was badly needed. In the case of Towie-Barclay, this was the most difficult decision to make concerning its restoration. In the end it was decided to add two further storeys, so a careful study of similar features on other castles was made to allow the new caphouse to be detailed as authentically as possible. Craig Castle, one of the group of similar castles mentioned above, was the principal source of inspiration.

39. Towie Barclay dates from the third quarter of the 16th century and is of L-plan layout, built for Sir Patrick Barclay. The upper two storeys were added during the restoration, replacing a previous structure removed during the 18th century. The lower floors are vaulted.

To realise a successful restoration from a ruin and achieve as much historical accuracy as possible, as many existing features should be retained as practicable. This is not purely to allow an accurate appearance but also to save valuable historical information *in situ* for any future consultation. Within the great hall at Towie-Barclay, which is classed as 'one of the noblest and imaginative of tower house interiors',[3] all the main dressed stones around the apertures in the walls were left unplastered. Externally too, all the quoins were left uncovered by harl. This stipulation was laid down by the Historic Buildings and Monuments Department, who provided grant aid for the restoration. Although these stones are dressed from the local red sandstone which is soft and prone to erosion, many of them carry cut mason's marks and the wish was to leave them uncovered. At one time all these stones would have been covered, with the exception of the door and window facings. The stone rib-vaulted ceiling would have been covered in plaster and painted, as can still be seen at Balbegno Castle, Kincardineshire. At Towie-Barclay this too, was left bare after the restoration as it was felt that what was lost in historical accuracy was compensated for by the exposure of masonry of such high quality. Although the dressed stones are straight along the finished edge, the remaining sides are of random outline so to stop the plaster short and allow it to follow the uneven outer edge producing a rounded hand-crafted appearance.

However, with an ever increasing number of ruined properties being bought, higher and higher sums are being offered. If the ruin, once purchased, has itself been a large financial outlay, an owner may not be prepared to spend an even larger sum purely for the sake of a restoration. As many of these properties are bought principally for their prestige and financial value, an authentically restored castle with all its drawbacks may be deemed insufficient reward for the capital outlay. In turn, this may lead to an unnecessary and tragic violation of a unique historical building through insensitive addition of 'luxury' features. When the motive for restoration is the joy of the building itself, or when financial benefit is not the main aim, it is the ruin which should dictate the best course of action to take. This will ensure the building is not historically compromised but is allowed to take shape in the most fitting manner.

Pitfichie Castle—History and Restoration

Pitfichie Castle lies one and a quarter miles north of the village of Monymusk, to the west of Kemnay. It lay ruinous for somewhere in the region of two hundred years before being bought and restored to its former glory.

In the fourteenth century, a charter of Pitfichie was granted to David Chalmers by David II, son of Robert the Bruce, thus creating Pitfichie as a secular estate, held from the Crown. Early in the fifteenth century, it passed to the Hurry family who were responsible for the construction of Pitfichie Castle. No precise date exists for its construction although it is thought to have been begun sometime in the 1560s. In 1716, the laird of Pitfichie died in exile after raising funds for the unsuccessful Jacobite rising of the previous year. None of his heirs sought to retain the estate and their castle birthplace was described as roofless in 1797. From this date no mention is made of Pitfichie until 1921.

In 1921, Dr W.D. Simpson, an eminent Scottish architectural historian, published the first and most comprehensive account[4] of the history of the castle. Simpson's account has been the basis for all subsequent work. A further report[5] by Simpson in 1949 stated that the castle was an 'irremediable ruin'. This conclusion had been reached as a result of the collapse of the majority of the east wall and south gable during a gale in 1936. Pitfichie was thus in this 'irremediable' state when Colin Wood first examined it with a view to restoration. An outline scheme was prepared for the restoration in the early 1970s and the Historic Buildings and Monuments Department was approached for grant funding. Initially this was turned down and proceedings ground to a halt. A few years later in 1975 the situation changed, funding became available, and Mr Wood finally bought the castle from Lady Grant of Monymusk in 1977.

Survey and preparations

The problems faced when undertaking a restoration from this ruinous state are complex. The first task is a thorough and detailed survey of the site and the existing structure. Special note is taken of any prominent features. Once drawn up, the survey is taken back to the site and double-checked. It provides a record of structural details which will inevitably be concealed in the course of the restoration. The drawings provide the foundation on which the details of the restoration are based.

As Pitfichie was so ruinous, and very little documentation existed as to its former state, the task of piecing together all the information and extant clues was a difficult and painstaking task. As much as possible of the detail for the project was obtained from sources dealing directly with Pitfichie, for example paintings and drawings. However, this gave but a fraction of the information required, and supplementary sources were consulted for background knowledge. Castles of a similar period were looked to for specific examples of contemporary detailing. Craigievar Castle was a major source of inspiration. Craigievar is an L-plan tower house, completed in 1626, built by the Bell family of master masons and is thought by many to be the most perfectly executed, unaltered and preserved example of a tower house in existence. Rowallan Castle and Brackie Castle were two further sources from which details were drawn.

Examining other castles for details, combined with a thorough knowledge of the reasons for the development of the tower house, its typical lay-out and the way the building functions, are the main guide-lines used to achieve an appropriate design. The gaps in the information which may still exist can only be filled through intuitive guesswork, and an understanding of, and sympathy for, the building. Upon this, the success of a restoration may depend.

At Pitfichie, an attempt was made to keep the restoration as authentic as possible, although certain concessions were made purely to improve the facilities within through modern heating and lighting.

Description and Restoration

The castle consisted of a rectangular tower house (10.9m–8.5m) forming the main block, with a circular tower 7.0m in diameter attached to its southern corner. A newel stair (1.2m wide) ascended between the main block and the tower, providing access to the upper storeys. The stair was corbelled out as a turret, lit by a gun-loop and small windows and, at the summit, was further enlarged by label corbelling, a popular ornamental device in the

40. Pitfichie is a mid-16th century rectangular tower house with a round tower tacked onto its southern angle. Access to the upper storeys is by newel stair crammed between the main block and the round tower. Pitfichie is probably a product of the prolific Bel family of master masons. Note the caphouse again sitting on label corbelling.

north of Scotland. Thus enlarged, the upper floor sat square on the
corbelling and formed a cap-house which rested on a vault above
the stairhead. The barrel-vaulted kitchen and cellar in the main
block were at basement level where the walls were 1.5m thick, with
the guardroom in the angle tower.

The process of restoration revealed that the angle tower is a
later addition to the original castle; several details point to this
conclusion. Firstly, the present position of the entrance door is not
original. The masonry inside shows that the former entrance was
in the west wall of the main block, complete with draw-bar tunnel.
A blocked-up arch, incorporating a gun-loop, now occupies this
former void. Secondly, fissures were to be seen in the masonry
between the main block and angle tower. These evidently opened
up as a result of settlement following the collapse of walling in
1936. There was no sign of any stones bonding the two elements
together, thus suggesting two independent phases of construction.
Thirdly, a line of slates was discovered in the chimney gable
stonework below the presumed original and present roof eaves
level, showing an addition had been made at some time. Lastly,
the position and orientation of the cap-house at the top of the stair
turret suggests, by its awkward angle, that it is a later addition.
However, in spite of these discoveries pointing to staggered dates
of construction, the decision was made to take the restoration from
the time at which the castle was last inhabited. This decision,
naturally, allows maximum preservation of the surviving existing
structure.

Above the basement level are two further levels plus a garret.
On the first floor of the main block is the hall. This measures 7.6m
by 6.7m, with a private room, usually known as the laird's room,
in the round tower.

Evidence also exists[6] that David Bel was present at Pitfichie in
1607. His family of master masons, apart from working at
Craigievar as already mentioned, also worked at Crathes, Fraser
and possibly Fyvie Castles. As there was a definite link between
Pitfichie and the prolific Bel school, the choice of Craigievar from
which to lift supplementary inspiration was an appropriate one.
Before beginning the restoration, local mason Mr Slessor Troup
was appointed. He had been involved in the restoration of Harthill
Castle (completed 1975).

Where the collapse in 1936 had led to settlement, the castle foundations had to be strengthened before any reconstruction was carried out. The cracks which had opened up between the main block and angle tower had to be stabilised, stitched and bonded together. This ancient weak point is now stronger than at any time in its existence.

Masonry

As so much of the stonework was missing, the task of finding replacement stone to match was daunting. As most of the east wall and south gable was no longer in existence, extensive remedial action was needed. The finished castle was to be harled, so a decision was made to build the missing walls up in high quality concrete blocks. This made for a more economical, practical and easily workable solution than rebuilding in masonry. Indeed, a major advantage of a concrete block cavity wall, built to the same depth and profile as the existing walls, was that it was possible to run all the services inside; thus the essential electrical wiring and sanitary piping was completely hidden from view whilst retaining the correct aesthetic.

The existing walls being field gatherings or 'heathens', stone for the necessary facings and mouldings was gathered over a long period of time from such diverse sources as salvage from demolished buildings to a local builder donating a quantity of pink granite. Permission was also obtained from the Forestry Commission to re-open and work Rorandle Quarry, in order to obtain the correct type of stone for the fireplace surrounds. This stone was hard, brittle and difficult to work.

As many as possible of the stone facings to the windows were retained, but many others needed to be cut afresh. Where bars across the windows had been originally sunk into the surrounding stone-work, the ingress of water and subsequent weathering had quite severely damaged these facings. Fortunately, enough of the principal or key stones had survived to allow exact copies or replicas to be made, or at least establish what would have been there. The new facings are in pink granite.

Possibly the major success in the category of masonry at Pitfichie was the rebuilding of the barrel vault of the original kitchen which is now the dining room. The mason, with centring provided by the joiners, managed to reconstruct the vault using local stone. This part of the project was so successful that it was decided to leave this vault unplastered, in contrast to the other in the basement. The upper part of the turnpike stair was restored using reconstituted stone newels, coloured to match the original existing pink granite.

Floors

The ground or basement floors are finished with Caithness flagstones, as is the first floor. To obtain the required quantity of stone from Caithness to floor Pitfichie, it had to be cut afresh from the quarry. Unused to such large orders, the quarry took two and a half years to fulfil the order. The floors above are timber beams with timber boarding above. Although oak beams would probably have been the original timber used, pitch pine beams are now in place. This is a good substitute as it has the same appearance and grain as oak, although not commonly used until much later. The beams were salvaged from old warehouse buildings destined for demolition.

The boarding is also of salvaged pitch pine, the nails removed and the wood left to dry before being cut into strips and re-used. It is nailed directly onto the beams, providing, as well as the floor, the ceiling below.

Slates

The slates came from the roof of a disused jute mill in Dundee which was being demolished. Whilst Foudland slates are perhaps more accurate or authentic for this part of Scotland, the decision was made to opt for Ballachulish slates which are harder and more durable.

Windows

In the single-glazed, sash and case windows which occur at all levels, bar the ground floor, a small sacrifice in authenticity for the sake of comfort has been made. Originally, as is shown in the existing stone facings around the apertures, the top section of the opening contained a fixed, leaded light. The grooves cut into the stonework for this light can still be seen. These windows are

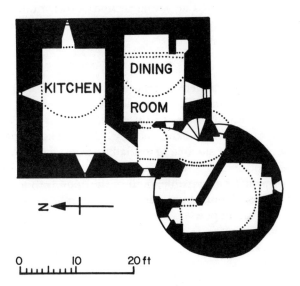

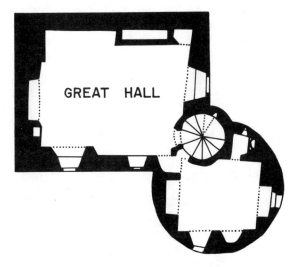

41. Upper: Pitfichie Castle—plan of ground floor.
Lower: Pitfichie Castle—plan of first floor.

not a complete anachronism as they did come into use in the eighteenth century. The actual section of their mullions is based on those at Craigievar.

Heating

Radiator pipe-runs were incorporated in the castle at the time of its restoration but no decision was made on the source of heat until later. Underfloor heating was briefly considered but was deemed too expensive to warrant further thought. Oil-fired heating was chosen, with a new boiler situated in a small cottage adjacent to the castle.

Radiators were carefully positioned inside in an attempt to intrude as little as possible, both in the appreciation of the castle itself and of the furniture within. The fireplaces throughout the castle are still in position and in working order to supplement the heating if required.

Walls

Internally, plaster on hard is the traditional finish for walls, which is then whitewashed. However, at Pitfichie the ruin had lain open to the elements for so long that the walls had become completely waterlogged. To plaster over this would have presented serious problems as an impervious coating would seal the moisture into the walls to the extent that it would eventually build up and escape, bringing the plaster down with it. To overcome this problem, a special renovating plaster was used. Once applied, this plaster allows the masonry beneath to breathe, giving the trapped moisture a non-damaging escape route.

Terpersie Castle: Historical background

Terpersie Castle lies four miles west of Alford sited deep in a glen in the Correen Hills. The castle was built in 1561 by William Gordon who, having purchased the lands from the Bishop of Aberdeen in 1556, set about building his castle. He was the fourth son of James Gordon of Lesmoir. The castle was strategically placed from the Gordon point of view as traditional rivals of the Forbes family in the midst of Forbes-controlled territory; an aggressive gesture in itself.

42. Terpersie Castle was described in the late in the 19th century as 'now in sad dilapidation'. This photograph of around that date confirms that assessment, but displays the castle's classic Z-plan layout, of which it is believed to be the earliest dated example in the North East. (From the George Washington Wilson Collection, University of Aberdeen.)

After the sixth laird, Charles Gordon, became the last Jacobite rebel to be executed for his part in the uprising of 1745, his family were turned out of Terpersie. The estate was bought by the York Buildings Company, which specialised in the exploitation of forfeited estates. At the end of the eighteenth century, the lands were purchased by another branch of the Gordon family, but Terpersie was only utilised as a farmhouse as the new owners lived at nearby Knockespock.

In a late nineteenth century account of the castle's condition, it was noted that it was 'now in sad dilapidation'.[7] Some fifty years later, it was noted by Dr W.D. Simpson as 'fast hastening to utter decay'.[8] It remained in a ruinous condition until 1982, when it was purchased from Mr Ian Fellowes-Gordon of Knockespock when a restoration was planned. Captain Lachlan Rhodes, formerly of the Gordon Highlanders, eventually chose Terpersie for restoration as a home.

Description and Restoration

Terpersie Castle is generally recognised as the earliest firmly dated example of a Z-plan tower house in Scotland. This fact made accurate restoration an essential priority.

The basic form of Terpersie Castle is of a rectangular main block with two diagonally-opposed subsidiary towers. The main block measures 8.5m by 5.4m and the towers are both 5.1m in diameter.

Although Terpersie is small, even 'diminutive in size',[9] its cunning in design is not reduced. Further, due to its presence in rival Forbes territory, it had to possess ease of defence and security. Its design satisfied those criteria admirably.

At basement or ground level, no windows existed. The only openings at that level were three gunloops in each of the towers and another four loops in the main block. Those in the towers are so arranged as to protect all flanks of the main block from within, with the remainder provided to cover both the towers and the surroundings. The basement level was 'completely arranged for defence by small arms'.[10] The walls at Terpersie are relatively thin, being 0.9m at basement level, and thus designed to withstand only musketry. Even in the sixteenth century, artillery was quite capable of penetrating this depth of masonry.

The main entrance door is not in a re-entrant angle between the main block and tower or jamb, as is more usual for tower houses, e.g. those at Towie-Barclay and Pitfichie. Instead the door is placed at the south end of the main block's eastern elevation. It is protected by one gun-loop in that same wall and by another in the north-east tower. Originally a yett may have protected the entrance, together with a sturdy wooden door.

At Terpersie, the basement is somewhat of a departure from the norm as far as construction is concerned. It was usual for tower-houses of this period to have a stone-vaulted basement. This was to give both a strong foundation on which to build the upper levels and adequate protection from fire and attackers. The basement level at Terpersie was not constructed like this. In the main block, the timber-beam floor of the hall above serves as the ceiling to the basement. The towers, however, are constructed as stone vaults at this level, being circular outside and crudely heptagonal within.

The basement level would have originally been used for storage and as an area to fend off attackers. Some castles housed the kitchen in the basement, but there is no evidence to suggest this was the case at Terpersie. It is probable that, as there would have originally been a barmekin, or courtyard wall, food preparation would have taken place in an associated outbuilding, only supplemented by the hall fireplace. The basement now houses a kitchen within the north-east tower, entered directly off the dining room in the main block, whilst the south-west tower is a utility room.

From basement level, a stair within the thickness of the southern gable ascends from the passage link in the main block to the south-west tower. This leads to the great hall at first floor level. The stair is lit through two loopholes, one at its head and one at its foot.

The great hall contains a fireplace in the east wall and three windows, one in each wall bar the south. The north-east tower houses the laird's room. This room was lit by two windows and also had a fireplace, garderobe (or toilet) and an aumbry within the wall for the safekeeping of valuables. In the corresponding first floor tower there is one window and two gun-loops providing light. From this level, a turnpike stair, corbelled out externally, ascends to the second and attic floor. The internal arrangements here are a close copy of the floor below.

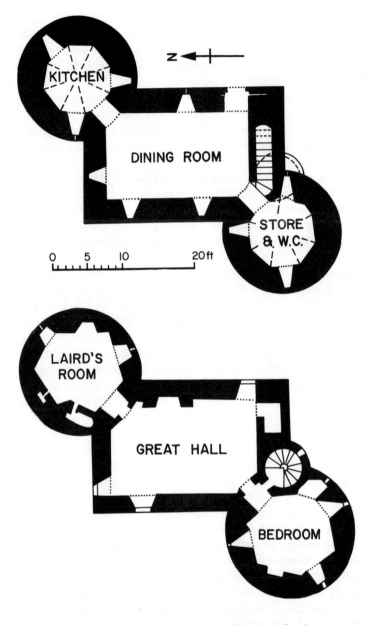

43. Upper: plan of ground floor at Terpersie Castle.
Lower: plan of first floor at Terpersie Castle.

A seventeenth century wing had been added to provide further accommodation at the east side of the main block. This wing had long since vanished to provide masonry for other buildings. The decision was made to omit this missing wing from the restoration. This was done partly to avoid any conflict with an otherwise perfect example of this particular type of castle and partly because no trace of it, except in drawings, now exists. Captain Rhodes enlisted the help of a former fellow army officer, Major Michael P. Taitt. Major Taitt was in the process of establishing a restoration-based firm of building contractors and agreed to undertake the project. Together they assembled a team to tackle the restoration. This included Mr Cowie, restoring architect at both Towie-Barclay and Pitfichie, and Mr Alistair Urquhart, a stone mason based at Aboyne. Grant aid was sought and obtained from the Historic Buildings and Monuments Department. After an initial survey, the architect could begin to piece together the original details of the design whilst the contractor undertook all the preparatory work on-site.

Once the rubble surrounding and filling the castle to a depth of about 1.2m had been removed, the building was again surveyed and all the newly discovered features incorporated in the design. Nothing survived above the great hall save one or two particular features, such as the remains of fireplaces, and window voids left isolated in the exposed walls.

Masonry

One of the first tasks to be undertaken, once the castle had been unearthed, was to give the existing masonry a steam cleaning. This dislodged and removed all the lichens and fungal growths which had developed, allowing a close examination of the underlying masonry. Some minor alterations to the plans were made once the overall condition of the structure was clearly known.

The existing walls at Terpersie were constructed of rubble. This technique involved using large, field-gathered stones, packed with smaller pinnings, with roughly dressed stones for the quoins. This type of construction was adopted because the materials were readily and freely available. The exterior was originally butter-pointed and harled with mortar leaving the larger stones exposed. The interior was plastered and white-washed.

A decision to use concrete blocks to repair the fabric of the walls was made for the same reasons of workability, non-appearance, cost and strength as at Pitfichie. The exterior would be harled, so the appearance of the new walling was unimportant, but the facings around the apertures, the corbelling and other masonry features were to be left exposed. The existing visible dressed stonework was in pink sandstone. The task of finding replacement sandstone of the correct shade was not easy and there was no short-cut. The contractor had to search it out piece by piece, each stone virtually being individually salvaged. From this recovered sandstone, new pieces were worked on-site by the mason for the door and window facings and lintels. The staircase, fortunately, was basically intact.

The external masonry was rendered with a roughcast of harl. The resulting light pink colour is known as 'Craigievar pink'. Many of the castles in this region, obviously including Craigievar itself, have a pink coloured harl. This is due to the red granite from which the aggregate was taken. At Terpersie, experiments were carried out with different ratios of this mix, to achieve exactly the desired shade of pink.

Floors

The basement floor has a flagstone finish, carried outside to form a small slabbed area around the entrance door. In the Tullynessle area, it was traditional that all the farmhouses were floored with the large flat stones quarried from the local Correen Hills and hence known as Correen flagstones. To reinstate the basement level in the authentic local material meant more salvage work for the builder, involving an extensive tour of the surrounding farms and houses to recover enough flagstones of the correct type to do the job.

The floor to the great hall is not of flagstone, as the absence of basement vaulting means that the existing structure is not strong enough to support such a weight. The first and second floors are timber beams resting on scarcements, with boarding fixed on top of this. Oak would have been the original timber employed, but a worthy substitute was found in pitch pine, as at Pitfichie. The beams were salvaged from an old paper mill. Beams which had already been in use, like those salvaged, were

44 (a). Terpersie Castle was designed with stone vaulting in the towers, but not the central block. As a secure home for the Gordon laird amidst hostile Forbes territory, its relatively thin walls and plethora of shot loops served only for small arms defence.

(b) The corbelled turnpike stair provided access from the hall to second and attic floor.

(c) During the restoration, the opportunity was taken to reinsert a window with construction date 1561 and the Gordon boar's head back into Terpersie's south gable. It had for some time been built into Knockespock House for safe keeping.

naturally aged, so giving the appropriate appearance. Salvage was also an economical method of obtaining timber of this span and section.

Windows

As at many other tower houses of that period, Terpersie had only gun-loops at basement level. At first floor level and above, windows provided light. Although, as the existing masonry shows, the apertures were originally designed to hold a leaded light and timber shutter arrangement, this was rejected. Timber sash and case windows were installed to give satisfactory protection from the elements and maximum daylighting. Despite this absence of exact sixteenth century authenticity, the appearance of the castle has lost none of its quality or charm.

The gunloops, although small, are the only source of light to the basement. They are plain, circular openings, between 11cm and 15cm in diameter, of dressed sandstone with a large internal splay. Plate glass and lime mortar have been used to glaze these apertures. Elsewhere there are vertical slit gun-loops which have been glazed in the same manner. In some cases a timber surround to the glass has also been employed. This expedient is the norm in restoration work.

Conveniently placed gun-loops in both the north-east and south-west towers, serve as kitchen extractor fan outlet and tumble drier vent outlet, respectively—a perfect example of acceptable compromise between sixteenth and twentieth century requirements.

Roof

In roofing the castle, large second-hand Scotch slates were sought and used. They were fixed in diminishing courses to the ridge. The eaves row of slates were 65cm broad which meant that to provide secure fixing, the slates were centre, rather than head nailed. The two conical roofs topping the flanking towers are actually oval on plan, thereby testing the skill of the slaters. At the eaves no rones are fixed which is in keeping with the period. This obviates the necessity for downpipes and leaves the elevations uncluttered, as at Pitfichie. Terpersie relies on the steep pitch of its roof to throw the rain-water clear of the face of the building. To avoid water-logging the ground in the immediate vicinity of the castle, clay drains were sunk to carry the rain-water away.

Doors and Hardware

The main entrance door has been constructed from oak fixed with iron nails. These are probably the original materials, but larch could have been an alternative timber.

The iron nails, ninety-nine of which secure the timber of the door together, were individually made by a local blacksmith. The nails, along with the door handle, escutcheon plate and bolt on the inside of the door were all fabricated from sketches of Major Taitt's designs. The entrance door is hung on its original iron hinges.

All the internal doors are also made of oak, with individual iron door hardware courtesy of the local blacksmith. Although they are not exact replicas of specific examples of ironmongery, after carrying out research into the subject, the designer has achieved an accurate aesthetic in materials appropriate for the period. The door is held shut against sandstone jambs and lintel, which, although smooth, cannot give a secure, airtight seal because no rebate or stop exists in the masonry, nor can one be inserted as this would be a major departure from original detail.

An attempt to solve the problem, using a synthetic foam seal around the inside of the jambs, as proved satisfactory at Pitfichie, has been made.

The Restoration of Fyvie Castle

The background and history concerning the development of Fyvie Castle is very complicated. Much has been written about its pedigree over the years, most recently by Mr H. Gordon Slade[11] and Mr Ian B.D. Bryce.[12]

Fyvie Castle differs in numerous ways from Towie-Barclay, Pitfichie and Terpersie and its inclusion here provides a contrast in scale and the nature of the problems faced.

The earliest known mention[13] of a castle at Fyvie on that site is in 1211, when William the Lion granted a royal charter from there. It is thought that William stayed there between 1211 and

1214. No evidence exists to show the form of that castle but it is probable that it was a timber structure at that time.[14] It is likely that by the time Edward I of England stayed at Fyvie, c.1296, the nucleus of the present castle was in existence, probably consisting of a rectangular courtyard castle, with four square angle towers and a gatehouse block. The castle was partially dismantled in 1308 by Robert the Bruce during the 'harrying of Buchan' which followed the defeat of the Earl of Buchan at Barra, near Old Meldrum.

In 1380, the castle was granted to Sir James Lindsay who was the nephew of the ruling monarch, Robert II, and in 1390 changed hands again to become the property of Lindsay's brother-in-law, Sir Henry Preston. The Meldrum family acquired the castle in 1430, and they probably continued to alter and add to the structure.

It was not until 1596, however, when Fyvie Castle was purchased by Alexander Seton, later 1st Earl of Dunfermline and Chancellor of Scotland, that it took on something of its present appearance. It is to Seton that we can attribute the central 'Seton Tower' in its present form, with its heraldic frontispiece and turreted cap-house over a flying arch. The upper works of the 'Preston' and 'Meldrum' towers, much work in the west range and the magnificent newel stair which terminates the latter, all date from this period. The traditional names given to the towers are a later romantic touch. Ninety years later, the 4th earl, grandson of the first, carried out minor alterations but due to his loyalty to the House of Stewart his estates were confiscated and he had to go into exile.

The property eventually came into Gordon ownership but remained empty and derelict until 1777. From this date General William Gordon embarked upon a programme of improvements which were completed by his illegitimate son before his own death in 1847. Perhaps the most remarkable surviving work of this period is the north-west or 'Gordon Tower', an eighteenth century replacement which accurately echoes the sixteenth century originals, an early instance of restoration. Also at this time a survey described the north and east ranges as 'ruinous vaults', which were removed thus destroying all surface evidence of the medieval courtyard.

The last Gordon laird was obliged to sell the estate and it was bought by Alexander Forbes-Leith, later to become Lord Leith of Fyvie in 1889. Although he had made his fortune in the steel industry in America, he had been locally born, and traced his ancestry back to Sir Henry Preston.

Lord Leith made his own impression upon the castle by extending the entrance hall; adding a further wing, the 'Leith Tower'; completely re-decorating the interior and acquiring paintings and other furnishings with Gordon associations. He died in 1926 and the castle, as it stands today, is virtually as Lord Leith left it. Fyvie Castle passed from the Forbes-Leith family when it was purchased by the National Trust for Scotland, with help from the National Heritage Memorial Fund, from Sir Andrew Forbes-Leith in 1984.

Description and Restoration

Since being acquired by the Trust, Fyvie Castle has undergone an extensive programme of restoration. The castle had been in the main continuously occupied over the past two hundred years whilst the building evolved so it was not ruinous. Thus the restoration of this castle, although still a major task, started at a considerably more complete point than at the other castles already described. It is an undertaking more realistically and accurately described as a 'repair' rather than a 'rebuild'.

The castle stretches 51m in length along its south range, an elevation dominated by the imposing twin drums of the central Seton Tower and terminated at either end by virtually identical towers, the Preston Tower to the east and the Meldrum Tower to the west. The west range projects 41m northwards from the Meldrum Tower until terminating against the Gordon Tower. Westward of the Gordon Tower is the fifth and most recent addition, the Leith Tower.

One of the first major requirements in the initial stages of the restoration was the removal of the harl from the south front. Fyvie had been re-harled in 1962, but for a combination of reasons, this work had been incorrectly and unsuccessfully carried out.

During this earlier renovation, the presence of ironwork built into the fabric of the castle was noted by Dr W.D. Simpson: 'The west gatehouse tower has, at some period, been strengthened by steel bands bolted into the masonry and of course concealed by the

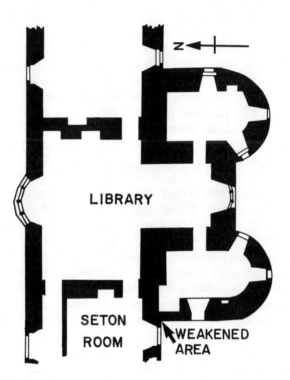

45. Fyvie Castle: plan of weak point where the Seton Tower meets the south range.

harling'.[15] As the 1962 renovation was limited to external works, it was not realised how extensive this strengthening actually was.

Under the supervision of Mr Alexander Mennie of McCombie and Mennie, architects, Inverurie, a detailed study of the steel banding was made. As the restoration was being part-funded by the Historic Buildings and Monuments, Scottish Development Department, there were certain stipulations made. One of these was that no ferrous metal was to be left within the structural fabric of the castle as, over a period of time, this would naturally weaken as it eroded. Careful consideration was therefore needed to ascertain the exact function of the steelwork and the effect of its removal. It was concluded that there were three independent systems of iron support for the west drum of the Seton Tower, inserted to counteract its westwards settlement. On analysis, the nature of the ironwork, structural members within the walls and under the floors, suggested major strengthening works had been undertaken, apparently designed prior to insertion and probably installed at a time when the castle had been unoccupied.

Iron work in the first system braces the west drum at the fourth floor level, tying it into the roof space and down to the third floor. The second system, independent of the first, embraces the drum and ties it back to the north wall of the south range. The third system, again independent of the others, braces and ties the west drum at first floor level to the main facade. Buttressing, applied to the west wall of the west range in the eighteenth century, is further evidence of an inclination to settle westwards.

Before looking at the solutions to the problems raised by these systems, it would be helpful to offer a brief explanation of their presence. At first floor level, at the point where the west drum of the Seton Tower meets the main south range, it is now evident that a considerable weakness has been caused. At the crucial point where the wall of the drum meets the main south wall, a chamber has been formed by cutting back into the walls, robbing the junction of essential strength. Adjacent to this chamber, again within the wall of the west drum, a fireplace has been cut. Although now blocked up, the original removal of stonework would also contribute to a localised weakness. Adjacent to the node point of the drum and the south facade, are a series of window apertures on the ground, first and second floor levels.

These voids, together with the former two instances of wall thinning, may well have sufficiently weakened the structure to result in settlement occurring and suggesting the need to install iron reinforcements to counteract the movement.

As was the practice, the external walls at Fyvie were constructed using field gatherings, this being the cheapest, most readily available material. This type of stonework, through its very nature and construction, was neither as strong nor as predictable as a coursed masonry wall of equivalent thickness. Bearing this in mind, the removal of the supporting ironwork might have proved disastrous if careful consideration had not been given to the provision of alternative strengthening.

The solution involved three broad means of remedial support. Each of these works alongside the others to stabilise the west drum of the Seton Tower.

It was decided that the best way to consolidate the masonry of the drum itself was to inject it with cement grout. This grout was mixed to a runny consistency and injected into the wall at approximately 500mm centres both horizontally and vertically. The mix used was in the ratio of one bag of cement to fifteen gallons of water. As this was so fluid, it flowed around within the thickness of the wall, plugging gaps and knitting the whole fabric of the wall together as it set. This was carried out working upwards from ground level.

Some problems encountered during this process included having the grout find its way through the wall and into the interior of the drum which, although empty at ground level, housed the Library annexe at first floor level. Unavoidably the annexe, which had just itself been completed in the refurbishment programme, had to be completely gutted to allow direct access to the inside of the masonry walls of the drum in order to seal them from further ingression of the grout. Before the grouting took place, the now unused flues of the Seton Tower were filled with dry cement to prevent the ingress of grout. Nine tons of cement were used for this. The drum was further strengthened by pouring an *in situ* concrete floor around a frame of stainless steel rods and into 'dovetails' cut in the masonry of the tower walls.

The processes described above helped to consolidate the masonry of the drum which was then further secured to the south range wall by stainless steel stitches.

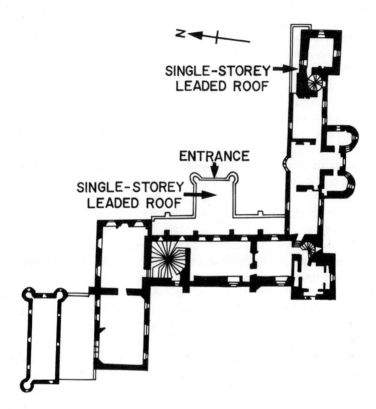

46. Fyvie Castle: plan of first floor.

When the harl had been removed from the chimney stacks of
the Seton Tower, it was discovered that when originally built, as
expected, no flue-liners had been used. As a result, over the
centuries, the carbon and smoke had eaten away and eroded the
soft sandstone. So far advanced was the erosion that the stone had
almost been eaten through so there was no alternative but to
rebuild the stacks to adequately support the heavy masonry
chimney caps.

Harl

With the harl removed, further discoveries emerged concerning
the south range. It became obvious that when the re-harling of
1962 had been carried out, it had been decided to harl right into
the window ingoes, stopping only at the timber of the window
frames themselves. This must have either been a conscious
decision or an oversight because, when the 1962 harl was
removed, dressed sandstone facings and surrounds were discovered around all the window apertures. It also became obvious
that the centre panel of the Seton Tower, between the two drums,
above the entrance door and below the connecting arch, was
constructed in fine sandstone with ashlar joints, hitherto concealed and forgotten.

When the harl was re-applied, these sandstone facings and the
ashlar central panel were left exposed, successfully revealing and
emphasising these features.

When it was realised that the re-harling of 1962 had been a
failure, careful consideration was given to the causes, in order to
avoid the same mistakes being made again. It was decided that,
because of the varied textures of stonework distributed over large
expanses of wall, with some upper areas having been constructed
hundreds of years later than others below, the present walls had
greatly differing properties and rates of absorption. This resulted
in some areas drying quicker than others, creating uneven
stresses, consequent cracking and eventually disintegration. It
was also thought that the sand used in the 1962 mix had been too
fine.

In fairness to the architects and contractors of that time it
should be borne in mind that this must have been one of the
earliest, and certainly amongst the largest re-harling projects

attempted in Scotland in the years following the Second World War.

To overcome the problems of this pioneering attempt, the walls were thoroughly picked and pointed before adding a 'scratch coat', a levelling coat of lean-mix cement, almost brushed into the wall, this being an attempt to cancel the effect of the different properties of the varied areas of the wall. A harled render, using a coarser sand in 1986, was then applied to this outer surface. No doubt this new exterior will be closely monitored for many years and, if successful, will become a model for structures with similar problems in the future.

Bell tower

As can be seen from engravings and paintings of Fyvie in the past, an octagonal bell tower, capped with a conical roof and weather vane used to adorn the central summit of the Seton Tower. By 1984, when purchased by the Trust, no bell tower existed. The date of its removal and subsequent loss had not been discovered but it was felt that the replacing of a tower on the then vacant leaded octagonal plinth could only add to the authenticity of the restoration.

The actual bell still existed, hung on the wall outside the entrance door of the west range, although as it was in sad need of repair it was sent off to the Whitechapel Bell Foundry in London to be refurbished.

Meanwhile, pictures and paintings were gathered and examined to ascertain the correct design and appearance of the original bell tower. The best source of illustration proved to be an article and accompanying photographs of Fyvie Castle, retrieved from the archives of *Country Life* magazine, dated 1912.

Sketches and models were made of the tower before a half-scale wooden mock-up was placed in position and photographed from a distance for comparison. Thus satisfied with the appearance of the proposed tower, a full-scale structure was made and lifted by crane, complete with bell and new weather vane, into position. Stainless steel dowels and epoxy resin adhesive hold the tower in place.

Leadwork

Although the large part of Fyvie's roofs are pitched and slated, there is a flat roof covering the single storey entrance hall and wing corridor of the west range. When the castle was purchased by the National Trust in 1984, it became obvious that this lead-covered flat roof area was in need of attention as it leaked.

The experts finally decided that the manner in which the roof had been sub-divided into bays to be leaded was quite correct in principal, but that at Fyvie the bays were too large. Flat lead roofing must endure extremes of temperature which result in expansion and contraction of the metal. If the areas are too large this flexing will stretch and warp the lead beyond the controlling limits of the wood rolls. Eventually this will cause failure in the lead. Adding to the dangers of this failure, the parapet gutter appeared to be too shallow and the down pipes too narrow. If and when the downpipes became clogged and blocked with a build-up of ice, water would not take long to fill up the already shallow gutter and flow back onto the lead roof. As the lead was already stretched and weakened, roof failure was frequent.

Apart from these faults, the gauge of lead used in the roof's manufacture appeared to be too thin. When the roof was renovated these details were rectified, a thicker gauge of lead in smaller sheets laid in smaller areas over more wood rolls. This allows greater and more rapid expansion and contraction. Vents were added to clear any moisture which might become trapped beneath the lead. To prevent a build-up of ice resulting in a damming effect which would flood the roof, electric heating elements, linked to automatic temperature sensors, were installed within the downpipes. This ensures they remain free of ice.

Although much of what has been noted applies to the south and west ranges and the Gordon and Leith Towers, there are further points which are more appropriately described in relation to the last named.

Masonry

Much of the decorative moulding and corbelling throughout the castle, as well as window facings and carved details such as coats of arms, have needed repair or replacement. The red sandstone

47 (a). Fyvie Castle, perhaps the most chateau-like of all the North East castles, is a composite structure, but essentially of 16th century date. Restoration and remedial activities carried out by the National Trust for Scotland have revealed some of its complex history.

(b). The octagonal bell tower at Fyvie which formerly sat on the Seton Tower has recently been replaced, using early 20th century archival photographs as a model.

which was originally used came from a local quarry near Turriff, long since defunct. This presented the problem of getting a supply of stone of suitable matching colour for the repairs.

The Stenhouse Conservation centre gave advice as to which stone, presently available, would be comparable with the original. From a short list of three, the choice fell upon one called Red Wilderness which is quarried in Gloucestershire. This stone was sent north in seven ton sections to the mason, Mr William Watson, in St Andrews. From these sections the mason carved and worked what he required for the repairs. Concerning the mouldings of the west range only those stones which were extremely badly damaged or eroded were replaced with new stone. This was in pursuance of the wise policy of leaving as much of the original work in place as possible.

Although appearing slightly odd at first, this method allows future restorers to calculate erosion rates and perhaps cut future replacement stones from the original templates. It also provides a visible indication of the condition of the masonry before repairs were undertaken. It has to be accepted that the new masonry appears stark by contrast, but natural weathering will ensure a much darker and more appropriate tone in a few years.

Where settlement has caused cracking or splitting in the sandstone facings around the windows, repairs have been very successfully carried out using epoxy resins. In some instances the damage was too great for repair, leaving replacement the only alternative.

Another interesting discovery awaited the restorers beneath the harl of the Leith Tower. From the second floor level of the west face there projects a large and intricately detailed oriel window, constructed of sandstone. On removal of the harling from the vicinity of this projecting feature, it was discovered that none of the masonry courses of the large window were actually built into the main west facade. At first examination it appeared as if the window was resting on thin air. Further investigation led to the discovery of an iron railway rail, or rails, which had been built into the masonry walls adjacent to the oriel and it is upon these that the entire stone structure is cantilevered out. The crack where the window butts against the main wall had been 'buttered' over with render to disguise the join.

To avoid the risky and complex task of removing these ferrous rails, with subsequent unpredictable results, it was agreed that on this occasion the rails, obviously an original and essential constructional device, could be left in place. Other instances of the same type of iron railway rail, used in similar load-bearing situations, have come to light in work carried out in the time of Lord Leith's tenure.

Conclusions

All restoration debate revolves around compromise. This is caused by the conflicting demands of historical accuracy and authenticity on one hand and contemporary convenience and comfort on the other. The theoretical ideal would be to make no compromise to comfort, but this would be impractical. Where castles are to be restored for habitation, a certain degree of compromise is always inevitable and often essential.

Each of the castles examined has a different character dependent, in part, on the degree of compromise made.

Towie-Barclay was the first of many castle restorations to take place in North East Scotland in the early 1970s. Of the four castles described, it is the most romantic in nature. This restoration was largely shaped by the Gothic nature of the groined and rib-vaulted great hall; a dramatic feature inspiring correspondingly rich re-building. Pitfichie was more recently restored, with a conscious effort made towards authenticity. This castle exudes an air of sensitivity, if not the same vibrancy as at Towie-Barclay, a discreet precision rather than bold strokes. Terpersie is the most recently completed restoration and is historically precise. Studious efforts were made throughout to recapture the mood of the original castle through the purity of its detailing.

Fyvie is still under restoration and thus cannot be compared using the same criteria. With its variety of architectural phases and present function as a National Trust property, its value ethos lie rather in the successive constructional developments than a return to correct observance appropriate to any one period. The discoveries made during its restoration have, however, ensured a greater awareness of the true nature of this highly complex building.

Where a departure has to be made from what is thought to be historically authentic, it should be handled as sympathetically as possible. Any such change should be reduced to absolute necessities or limited to areas where a certain amount of compromise will be inoffensive. This point can be illustrated by recalling how the missing stone stairs at Pitfichie were replaced by reconstituted stone, a compromise which does not in any way detract from the overall success of the restoration. Where no evidence has survived to enable the restoration design to be completed as the original, sensitive interpolation coupled with appropriate plagiarism may provide the required pattern. This was the manner in which the design of the cap-house at Towie-Barclay was obtained.

Twentieth century additions and amenities exist in each castle alongside the existing ancient fabric. At Terpersie no effort has been made to disguise the low-voltage spotlights which provide essential artificial light. Whilst clearly not an original feature, their design allows an immediate visual disassociation with them, allowing the otherwise authentically renewed interior to be viewed without hindrance. At Towie-Barclay, iron light fittings have been fashioned to disguise their modernity. Thus at Terpersie there is a straight-forward and honest addition of artificial light; at Towie-Barclay, a sensitive imitation.

In certain situations a complete departure from historical veracity is perfectly admissible and has no ill-effects on the restoration. All of the restored ruins had walling rebuilt in concrete block where exterior and interior cladding would conceal such material. This compromise has the advantage of being an indisputable indication for future restorers as to the extent of twentieth century work. Restorers must consider the future as well as the past.

It must also be noted that a respect for the building or ruin, as found, must be exercised. That is to say, it would be wrong to select an isolated moment in history and restore only to that point, unless, of course, it would be detrimental to the project to do otherwise. For example, the windows in the great hall at Towie-Barclay had been previously enlarged, so it would have been pointless to reduce them again. The later tower at Pitfichie is more appropriate in place than demolished to allow the original main block to stand alone. The reverse is true where Terpersie is concerned where the rebuilding of the later wing would have impaired the qualities of the classic Z-plan as it was originally conceived. At Fyvie, it cannot be denied that a disregard for the efforts of a previous restoration has allowed the present scheme to expose striking features once again for all to see.

To restore a sixteenth century tower house for occupation requires, apart from time and money, also determination, devotion and flexibility. Tower houses, before restoration, are cold, dark, and waterlogged after years of neglect as ruins. After restoration they may no longer be cold, given adequate heating, or dark, given adequate lighting; but they will remain damp for some years to come, although this will diminish in the course of time. As a result of its design a tower house means many stairs to ascend or descend to gain access throughout the building in the course of normal daily life, each domestic function still having to be dealt with at a different level.

A combination of prior awareness and willingness to adapt is needed to accept the building as it is, with all its disadvantages in twentieth century terms, and an empathy which enables the resident to live within the terms dictated by the castle itself. Some sacrifices must be made to the fabric and structure of the castle to enable a modern lifestyle, with its assumed amenities, to be located within the original shell. As authenticity is foremost, the design planning of the restoration is largely dictated by the original layout, or is a close approximation. For example, the former cellars of Terpersie now house a kitchen and dining room, adequate for the present owner but not for the larger household of the original laird; the cap-house of Towie-Barclay includes a library and recording studio; the former kitchen of Pitfichie has been re-created as the dining room and the kitchen is now in a former cellar.

It is not that the original plan arrangements in any of the examined tower houses did not function adequately in their time, just that after two or three hundred years a different layout is required. The main aim of these restorations was to preserve a piece of history as far as possible, which would have otherwise descended into a ruin beyond repair as at Pitfichie or where 'soon there will be no occasion to visit its peaceful site'[16] as was once said of Terpersie.

As well as the day-to-day co-ordination of the basic restoration work, the architect has a more subtle role to play. It is his duty to look after the best interests of the castle, as well as his client, the silent but expressive structure as well as the vocal and financially-liable human. The architect has to protect the building from exploitation, insensitive addition and inappropriate alteration. To do this he (or she) must be equipped with a thorough knowledge of the appropriate models for this major national building type. As restoration continues this is both easier, because there are an increasing number of completed examples of previous exercises available for study. and more difficult, because there must be a decreasing number of potential restorers prepared to accept the limitations imposed by such buildings.

Another difficulty facing the architect is to gain a building warrant for the proposed work. When these castles were originally constructed the standards now accepted as normal and essential were unknown. There are thus numerous areas where the proposition will automatically fail to comply with building regulations. Yet it is imperative that a degree of relaxation of such regulations is accepted in order to retain the desired character of the building.

It was noted less than fifty years ago, as somewhat of a tragedy, that so many picturesque and historic buildings were doomed to slow disintegration and disappearance.[17] Since that was written more than forty castles have been restored to habitation in the Grampian Region alone. These rescue operations, whilst of varying degrees of success, nonetheless ensure a strong castle presence for many years to come. All these restorations have, to a greater or lesser extent, attempted to reproduce a historically accurate building.

It is a glowing testament to the successful designs of the original masons that a desire still exists to preserve and inhabit these fascinating and ancient Scottish tower houses in preference to anything the twentieth century has to offer.

REFERENCES

1. Part of a thesis presented to Robert Gordon's Institute of Technology towards a BSc. Honours Degree in Architecture, 1990.
2. S. Cruden, *The Scottish Castle* (London, 1963), 165.
3. Ibid., 166.
4. W.D. Simpson, 'Notes on five Donside castles', *Proceedings of the Society of Antiquaries of Scotland*, 55, 1921, 133–39.

5. W.D. Simpson, *The Earldom of Mar* (Aberdeen, 1939), 122–25.
6. *Register of the Privy Council of Scotland* (Edinburgh, 1607), 8, 635.
7. D. MacGibbon and T. Ross, *The castellated and domestic architecture of Scotland* (Edinburgh, 1882), vol.2, 208.
8. W.D. Simpson, 'Two Donside castles', *Proceedings of the Society of Antiquaries of Scotland*, 66, 1942, 93.
9. D. MacGibbon and D. Ross, op.cit., 205.
10. R.W. Billings, *The baronial and ecclesiastical antiquities of Scotland* (Edinburgh, 1852), vol.4, 56.
11. H. Gordon Slade, 'Fyvie castle, Aberdeenshire, Scotland', *Chateau Gaillard*, 12, 1984, 151–56.
12. I.B.D. Bryce, 'The development of Fyvie castle', *Aberdeen University Review*, 173, 1985, 74–82.
13. H. Gordon Slade, op.cit., 152.
14. W.D. Simpson, 'Fyvie castle', *Proceedings of the Society of Antiquaries of Scotland*, 73, 1938, 44.
15. W.D. Simpson, manuscript, 21 May, 1962, 41 (Special Collections, University of Aberdeen).
16. I.B.D. Bryce, 'Terpersie castle', *Leopard Magazine* (Aberdeen, February, 1976), 15.
17. W.D. Simpson, op.cit., (1942), 93.

GLOSSARY

butter pointing = flush pointing.

entasis = the swelling outline of a column or building.

escutcheon = shield on which coat of arms is represented.

gunloop = a small narrow aperture principally for shooting through but also allowing limited ventilation and daylight penetration.

heathens = stone gathered from the surface of the ground, used for rubble walling.

heptagonal = seven sided.

jamb = straight upright side post of a doorway or side of an arched window.

mullion = the upright division between the lights of a window.

newel = the upright column about which the shape of a circular staircase winds.

oratory = a small private place of worship.

oriel window = polygonal protruding window supported on corbels.

quatrefoil = open tracery shaped as a four-lobed flower.

quoins = large, dressed corner stones at the junction of two wall surfaces.

scarcement = ledge.

scratch coat = a cement rendering which has its surface both grooved and raised to provide a base to which harling can adhere.

wattle and daub = interlaced rods and twigs plastered with mud or clay used in the construction of primitive fences, walls and roofs.